I0069095

Edinburgh Law Essentials

# SCOTTISH LEGAL SYSTEM ESSENTIALS

# EDINBURGH LAW ESSENTIALS

*Series Editor*: Nicholas Grier, Abertay University, Dundee

*Scottish Administrative Law Essentials*
Jean McFadden and Dale McFadzean

*Medical Law Essentials*
Murray Earle

Property Law Essentials
Duncan Spiers

*European Law Essentials*
Stephanie Switzer

*Intellectual Property Law Essentials*
Duncan Spiers

*Media Law Essentials*
Douglas Maule and Zhongdong Niu

*International Law Essentials*
John Grant

*Employment Law Essentials*
Jenifer Ross

*Human Rights Law Essentials*
Valerie Finch and John McGroarty

*Planning Law Essentials*
Anne-Michelle Slater

*Company Law Essentials*
Josephine Bisacre and Claire McFadzean

*Jurisprudence Essentials*
Duncan Spiers

*Trusts Law Essentials*
John Finlay

*Contract Law Essential Cases*
Tikus Little

*Succession Law Essentials*
Frankie McCarthy

*Commercial Law Essentials*
Malcolm Combe

*Revenue Law Essentials*
William Craig

*Private International Law*
David Hill

*Scottish Family Law*
Kenneth McK. Norrie

*Scottish Contract Law Essentials*
Tikus Little

*Public Law Essentials*
Jean McFadden and Dale McFadzean

*Legal Method Essentials for Scots Law*
Dale McFadzean and Lynn Allardyce Irvine

*Scottish Criminal Law Essentials*
Claire McDiarmid

*Roman Law Essentials*
Craig Anderson

*Scottish Environmental Law Essentials*
Essentials
Francis McManus

*Scottish Evidence Law Essentials*
James Chalmers

*Delict Essentials*
Francis McManus

*Scottish Legal System Essentials*
Gerard Keegan

www.edinburghuniversitypress.com/series/ele

Edinburgh Law Essentials

# SCOTTISH LEGAL SYSTEM ESSENTIALS

## 4th Edition

Gerard Keegan, B.A. (Hons), LL.B., M.Sc., Dip. L.P.
*ISC, University of Strathclyde*

EDINBURGH
University Press

*This book is dedicated to my three young brothers,*
*Lawrence, Bryan and Desmond Keegan.*

Edinburgh University Press is one of the leading university presses in the UK. We publish academic books and journals in our selected subject areas across the humanities and social sciences, combining cutting-edge scholarship with high editorial and production values to produce academic works of lasting importance. For more information visit our website: edinburghuniversitypress.com
© Gerard Keegan, 2021

First edition published <1st Edn Date>

Edinburgh University Press Ltd
The Tun – Holyrood Road
12 (2f) Jackson's Entry
Edinburgh EH8 8PJ

Typeset in 10/13 Bembo by
IDSUK (DataConnection) Ltd

A CIP record for this book is available from the British Library

ISBN 978-1-4744-6646-2 (hardback)
ISBN 978-1-4744-6648-6 (webready PDF)
ISBN 978-1-4744-6647-9 (paperback)
ISBN 978-1-4744-6649-3 (epub)

The right of Gerard Keegan to be identified as the author of this work has been asserted in accordance with the Copyright, Designs and Patents Act 1988, and the Copyright and Related Rights Regulations 2003 (SI No. 2498).

# CONTENTS

# TABLE OF CASES

# TABLE OF STATUTES

# WEBSITE REFERENCES

**Negative procedure**: www.parliament.uk/site-information/glossary/negative-procedure/

**Prisoner voting in the United Kingdom and Scotland – rights v political reality**: https://spice-spotlight.scot/2018/06/20/prisoner-voting-in-the-uk-and-scotland-rights-vs-political-reality/

**Supreme Court jurisdiction**: www.supremecourt.uk/docs/a-guide-to-bringing-a-case-to-the-supreme-court.pdf

# ACKNOWLEDGEMENTS

I would first like to thank Professor Bryan Clark, now of the University of Newcastle, for the confidence, encouragement and friendship that he has shown towards me. Thanks too to Sarah Naismith and colleagues in the ISC at the University of Strathclyde for their interest shown in the writing of this fourth edition. Similarly, my neighbour Jim Carey, if only because each time he asked about progress he reminded me of the deadline!

Thanks also to Tommy Bradshaw, retired Lanarkshire solicitor, for his inspiration; my wife Kathleen and son Thomas Rooney for their unstinting love and support; and Commissioning Editor Laura Williamson and Managing Desk Editor Fiona Conn at EUP for their behind-the-scenes assistance in bringing this latest edition of the *Scottish Legal System Essentials* to publication.

# 1 INTRODUCTION AND HISTORICAL DEVELOPMENT

To locate Scots law in its wider context it is worth appreciating that the Scottish legal system can be classified as 'mixed'. This is because the Scottish legal system lies somewhere between two classic types of legal regime: 'civil law' (or 'civilian') and 'common law'.

Under civil law codified statutes and ordinances are prevalent. While generally in common law jurisdictions previous legal precedents or judicial rulings are used to decide cases.

## CIVIL LAW AND COMMON LAW

Civil law systems are derived historically from Roman law and are commonplace in continental Europe. Common law systems, by contrast, are drawn from English law found in England, but also in Commonwealth nations and many US states.

The two schools may be distinguished in that civil law systems are based upon legal *deduction*, or rules deduced through general principles originally expounded by legal scholars, whereas common law systems are founded upon legal *induction*, or the formation of legal principles induced through court decisions in certain instances.

The terms 'civil law' and 'common law' can be confusing in that they also hold further meanings, aside from those described above. The term 'civil law' can also be used to denote law that, in general, regulates relations between private individuals in particular circumstances, such as contract law, property law and delict (essentially, negligence law in Scotland). This is opposed to criminal law, where a minimum moral standard of behaviour is laid down by the state that prohibits certain activities, such as murder, rape, assault and theft, by their classification as criminal acts. Moreover, the term 'common law' can be used to denote law which is non-statutory in nature (i.e., principles developed primarily through the courts, not out of legislation). As will be discovered, much of Scots law is rooted in such common law principles (see Chapter 2).

## PUBLIC LAW AND PRIVATE LAW

In terms of other classifications, Scots law can also be split into public law and private law. Public law comprises those legal rules which relate specifically to the state. Public law examples include constitutional law and administrative law, which set out rules pertaining to the powers of the organs of the state and govern the ability of the state in all its forms to regulate the lives of the public. Private law covers law that does not pertain specifically to the state. This division between private and public law has its roots in early Roman and Greek law and has long been recognised. The division is not however clear-cut, and some commentators have questioned its value, since there is no essential difference between the respective sources of private and public law, nor the procedure or courts in which rights thereunder are determined.

## A 'mixed' system

In relation to schools of law, the legal system in Scotland is interesting in that it exhibits features of both the civil law (Roman) and common law (English) systems (although in its present form it probably leans more towards the common law model). The fact that the Scottish system is 'mixed' in this way is no curious anomaly. Even a cursory analysis of the historical development of Scots law reveals significant influences from both sides of the legal school divide that have left an indelible imprint upon today's Scottish legal system. Indeed, our legal system has a rich and varied heritage and a somewhat colourful history. While a detailed exposition of the historical journey of the legal system in Scotland is beyond the scope of this short book, a summary of its evolution and key influences is set out below.

## HISTORICAL DEVELOPMENT

### Early English (Norman) influence

The origins of any legal system typically coincide with the emergence of a nation. Scotland emerged as a nation, broadly speaking, after the Battle of Carham, thought to be either in 1016 or 1018. In general, this brought together four separate tribes of peoples: the Picts, arguably Scotland's indigenous peoples; the Scots, a tribe of Irish descent; the Angles, a Germanic tribe brought to the border provinces by the Romans to help stabilise the region; and the Britons, a tribe which originally settled in what is now the west of Scotland.

While the laws of that time were largely customary and their development sporadic, the first major influence on the fledgling Scottish legal system occurred in the mid-eleventh century as a result of English 'feudalism' (an idea imported to England by the Normans after the Battle of Hastings in 1066). The high watermark of English feudal influence occurred during the reign of King David I, who ruled in Scotland from 1124 to 1153. David had spent much of his early life in England and, impressed by its system of governance, imported feudalism into Scotland, as well as other early English legal institutions such as the office of 'sheriff', which has, interestingly, endured to this day.

## Feudalism

Feudalism is essentially a system of landownership, its underlying and fundamental premise being that all lands belong to the Crown (monarch). The Crown would then grant or '*feu*' land in its territory to noblemen in return for 'feu duties', such as monetary payments, military allegiance and other forms of service. In turn, these noblemen ('tenants-in-chief' in receipt of lands from the Crown) would then feu parts of *their* land to others known as 'vassals', in return for feu duties from them. Land held by vassals could then be 'sub-feued' and split into yet smaller parcels and feued to others – a 'feudal pyramid' resulted, with the monarch firmly at the top.

From this pyramidal feudal structure developed not only a form of landownership but a system of top-down societal governance and control. This distribution of political power was bolstered as the tenants-in-chief (or 'barons') developed courts on their lands within which they settled claims and meted out justice. A king's court was also set up to disseminate the monarch's power and Sheriff Courts were established across the land to administer civil and criminal justice on behalf of the king. The sheriff's role in each part of the country was overseen by the monarch's 'justiciars', king's court officials who, on the Crown's behalf, were given extensive judicial powers in both criminal and civil matters. Over time the role of the justiciar fell away, but their jurisdiction in criminal proceedings can be seen as a forerunner to the development of Scotland's supreme criminal court – the High Court of Justiciary, established in 1672 – which remains in place to this day.

## Norse law

From as early as the middle of the ninth century, the land that was to become Scotland became subject to repeated attacks from Scandinavian forces over many centuries. Although Scotland was never conquered, as such, the Viking raiders did establish settlements in western and northern areas of Scotland such as the Hebridean Isles, Orkney and Shetland. As a result, these island areas became heavily influenced by Norse law and custom. Some of this

influence, most notably 'udal law' – the law pertaining to landownership –
has survived into modern times.

## Canon law

Aside from the courts described above, from the middle of the twelfth
century, the Canon law of the Roman Catholic Church began to exert
its influence. Church courts dealt principally with family law and
related matters, with their decisions commonly reviewed in Rome.
These courts continued to exercise jurisdiction up to the time of the
Scottish Reformation in 1559 when the Church's judicial functions
were abolished in Scotland and any further influence of Canon law
waned. Nevertheless, certain areas of Scots law (in particular, family
law), still to this day bear the hallmarks of much of this early ecclesias-
tical influence.

## Roman law

The historical influence of Roman law occurred in several ways. The
infiltration of Roman law into Scotland began in the middle of the
sixteenth century when, with scant opportunity for the study of law
at Scottish universities, Scots law students travelled to France and later
to the Netherlands for legal instruction. Given that Roman law had
been widely received across continental Europe at this time, on return-
ing home and being faced with issues in which there were no applicable Scottish legal principles, Scots lawyers naturally fell back on their
Roman law learning and principles to fill in the gaps.

## Advent of the Court of Session

Another key event in the influence of Roman law occurred in 1532 when
the first permanent civil (non-criminal) court in Scotland – the Court
of Session – was established. Based on a Roman model, the judiciary
that manned this institution had been educated primarily in Roman and
Canon law and consequently the effect of these schools of legal thought
permeated as the operation of the court settled. The Court of Session still
endures to this day albeit in a different form.

## Institutional writers

As the court began to mature, so too did legal writing become increasingly important. Beginning in the mid-seventeenth century, and continuing over the next 150 years or so, a substantial body of work was

produced by eminent legal scholars known today as 'institutional writers'. As will be seen in Chapter 2, these seminal works became so revered and influential that they began, in themselves, to represent a valid source of law. They were instrumental in charting the development of Scots law as it moved into a more modern age. Many of these early jurists were schooled in Roman law and hence their work, while drawing upon several influencing factors, often bore the hallmarks of Roman law.

## English law: the dominant modern influence

Although Roman principles continued to be expounded in institutional writings until the early nineteenth century, the beginning of the demise of Scotland's affinity with Roman law began with the Act of Union 1707.

A partnership borne largely out of economic and political expediency rather than mutual affection, the Act of Union brought about the amalgamation of the respective *Parliaments* in Scotland and England. The *Crowns* of Scotland and England had already been amalgamated in 1606 when James VI of Scotland ascended the English throne as James I of England. A crisis later arose when the last of the Stewart dynasty, Queen Anne, died without leaving an heir. Bitter disagreement between Scotland and England ensued as to who should ascend the throne. Neither country was able to accept war as a viable option at that time – England was at war with France; and Scotland was desperately impoverished and dependent upon continued trade links with its southern neighbour. Hence, an agreement was reached between the two countries that Scotland would recognise Sophia of Hanover as successor to the throne, and in return England would grant freedom of trade to the Scots. The treaty also entailed the union of the two parliaments.

## Legal implications of the Act of Union 1707

Despite mass protests on the streets of Scotland's cities, the incumbent Scottish Parliament that had developed as an offshoot of the Crown in the mid-fifteenth century was abolished along with its English counterpart, and the new Parliament of Great Britain was established at Westminster.

Importantly, under the Act of Union 1707, Scotland was deemed entitled to retain its own independent legal system and distinct Scottish laws – an exception being that English revenue law would apply to Scotland. By virtue of the terms of the Act, however, the laws of Scotland could now in general be amended by any new legislation passed by the Westminster Parliament. Consequently, any new laws enacted at Westminster would automatically become binding upon the Scottish people and the

Scottish court. This overrode any contrary Scottish common law (non-statutory) principles that had hitherto developed, and any contrary acts of the old Scottish Parliament. In addition, shortly after the Act of Union, the English-dominated House of Lords (sitting as a court) quickly assumed the role of hearing appeals on Scottish (non-criminal) civil matters from the Court of Session. This laid the foundations for English law to become the predominant influencing factor in Scotland over the next three centuries.

More specifically, as commerce and industry began to develop during the eighteenth century, Scotland began to adopt English commercial and mercantile laws, which were much more mature than their incumbent Scottish equivalents. The Napoleonic Wars of the early 1800s frustrated the ability of budding Scots lawyers to study at universities in continental Europe. In addition, the concurrent Industrial Revolution led to increased parliamentary activity and the enactment of an unprecedented amount of statutory legislation to regulate increasingly complex social norms, working methods and technologies such as the Factory Act 1833 and the Mines Act 1842. The bulk of this new legislation – often codified and built upon English common law, and now extending across the whole of Britain – washed away many previously distinct Scots social practices in the process. Similarly, principles of Scots law began to dissolve in a number of areas as a result of the increasingly heavy-handed influence of the House of Lords (sitting as a court) that overruled a series of Scottish civil law decisions of the Court of Session, arguably by the erroneous imposition of English doctrines.

Students of Scots law may be aware of an antipathy, that has existed since the Act of Union 1707, towards English law in certain Scottish legal circles, particularly in respect of its domination of much of Scots law and its replacement with English principles. Nevertheless, today, one should perhaps not lose sight of the fact that the origin of any law is not of much import when compared to the quality of that legal principle. We should be proud of our legal heritage and be wary of the importation of inferior legal doctrines; but we might pose the question that if a law is crafted to be fair and reasonable, logical, efficient, enforceable in practice and fulfils a societal need, should its historical origin be of any consequence?

## The European Union

While English law can be considered the major modern influence on the development of Scottish law, more recent political events have brought to bear new impacts on the Scottish legal system – and will continue to do so. In particular, European Community law (EC law) has played a significant role since the United Kingdom joined the (then) European Economic Community (EEC) in 1973, when the European Communities Act 1972 was passed to give effect to EC law within the United Kingdom. Suffice to say, that to the disquiet of some commentators and to the glee of others, in the pursuit of the harmonisation of laws across EC Member States, Scots law (and that of the United Kingdom as a whole) has in the past been increasingly superseded in a number of policy areas, including, for example, in the commercial, financial and employment spheres.

The legislation and legislative process of the (now) European Union are discussed in Chapter 2, along with a discussion on the European Union Referendum Act 2015, the outcome of which saw the United Kingdom voting to leave the European Union following the UK–EU membership referendum on 23 June 2016. Despite our decision to leave the European Union on the 31 January 2020, EU law will continue to have some import in the United Kingdom after our departure. First, expressly in the anticipated 'transition phase' after the United Kingdom's official departure on 31 January 2020; and impliedly thereafter, because of EU rules and regulations concerning trade.

## The revival of Scots law: the Scottish Parliament

In contrast to the demise of distinct Scottish principles since the Act of Union 1707, the late twentieth century saw a re-emergence in several policy areas of distinct and separate Scottish legal rules. This occurred because of the advent of the Scottish Parliament at Holyrood in Edinburgh. The new Scottish Parliament was created following the 'Campaign for a Scottish Assembly' launched in 1988, whose declared aim was the establishment of a new legislative body for Scotland and consequently the ensuing transference of power back from London.

It is perhaps somewhat paradoxical then, that the Scottish Parliament itself was created by a piece of Westminster legislation – the Scotland Act 1998.

## The Scotland Act 1998

The Scotland Act was passed following a referendum in Scotland in 1997, wherein the Scottish people voted in favour of its new devolved body, the Scottish Parliament. Since its inception, the Parliament has been empowered to legislate for its people in 'devolved' policy areas.

The extent to which this amounts to any real 'revival' of Scots law is debatable, and the Scottish Parliament has, at best, received a mixed reception over its first twenty-one years or so. Nevertheless, the inception of the

Scottish Parliament has certainly led to a parting of ways with English law in areas such as freedom of information, the sale of alcohol, drink-driving limits, sex-education policy within schools and anti-smoking legislation. The composition, work and legislation of the Scottish Parliament as a source of Scots law are considered in Chapter 2.

---

### Essential Facts

- Scots law is a mixed legal system, which means that it has been influenced by both classic legal schools: the common law system, derived from England; and the civil law system, derived from Roman law.
- The Scottish legal system has a rich heritage and has been influenced by several historical factors, including feudal law (from England), Canon law (of the Roman Catholic Church), Roman law, English law and European Community (EC) law.
- The early key influences were: feudalism (a system of landownership) and other governance tools borrowed from England, beginning in the eleventh century; Roman law, stemming from the foreign travel of law students, beginning in the sixteenth century; and the works of institutional writers, which were penned in the seventeenth, eighteenth and nineteenth centuries.
- More modern key influences include English law, which stemmed largely from legislation passed in the aftermath of the Act of Union 1707 and the influence of the Judicial Committee of the House of Lords (now the Supreme Court of the United Kingdom); and EU law, which has become increasingly important since the United Kingdom joined the European Economic Community in 1973.

## Website resources

**Scots law**

Wikipedia

https://en.wikipedia.org/wiki/Scots_law

**History of Scots law**

Wikipedia

https://en.wikipedia.org/wiki/History_of_Scots_law

**The legal system of the United Kingdom**

Chartered Institute of Legal Executives

www.cilex.org.uk/about_cilex/about-cilex-lawyers/what-cilex-lawyers-do/the-uk-legal-system

**'How do legal systems differ from one country to another?'**

*The Personal Injury Brief Update Law Journal*

www.pibriefupdate.com/content/pibulj-sec/2065-how-do-legal-systems-differ-from-one-country-to-another

## Video resources

**Scots law**

https://youtu.be/QS1cu609rk4

# 2 SOURCES OF SCOTS LAW

The term 'source of law' can hold different meanings. As noted in Chapter 1, Scots law has evolved over the best part of 1,000 years, being influenced by unsophisticated customary rules, Canon (or church) law, Roman law, feudal law and English law. The notion of a 'source of law' may also relate to the rationale behind the inception of a legal rule. In this sense, religious doctrines, social trends, political expediency and economic efficiency may underlie the adoption of legal principles.

Although these historical and philosophical influences account for the origins of Scots law, they do not answer the question as to why particular rules are binding upon us. If a rule is to be binding then it must be derived from one or more recognised sources of law, known as 'formal sources'. These formal sources are discussed below.

## FORMAL SOURCES

The formal sources of Scots law include:

- legislation; and
- common law.

Common law sources encompass:

- judicial precedent;
- institutional writings;
- custom; and
- equity.

## LEGISLATION

Legislation may be considered the primary source of law and is typically the result of the expression of the will of a rule-making body that exhibits some form of state legitimacy or authority. The volume of legislation affecting Scotland has increased considerably over recent years. Modern society is complex and, in reflecting this, the Westminster Parliament and now the Scottish Parliament have deemed it necessary to regulate and facilitate our multifarious activities by way of legislation.

Beginning during the Industrial Revolution in the 1850s, successive governments found it necessary to propose laws in areas such as employment, housing, health and social services, education and the environment. Current trends show no sign of the legislative juggernaut abating, leading some to claim that we now live in a nanny state, where Parliament has become increasingly guilty of over-regulating our lives. Recently, there has also been an increase in the number of bodies empowered to legislate for the people of Scotland. This power to legislate arises either constitutionally or, increasingly, by empowering legislation (known as 'delegated legislation'). Those bodies empowered to enact laws applicable to Scotland include the UK Parliament; the Scottish Parliament; until 31 December 2020, the European Union; and various individuals and organisations who are delegated the right to do so.

## UK legislation

### Constitutional issues

Th UK Parliament in Westminster was first established in 1707. The Parliament is *bicameral* in nature, which means that it comprises two legislative houses – the elected House of Commons and the non-elected House of Lords. Parliament (the Legislature) should be distinguished from the Government (the Executive). In short, the role of the Executive – which is headed by the Prime Minister and their ministerial Cabinet – is to propose new legislation, while Parliament's role is to enact it.

Unlike other jurisdictions, there is no strict separation of powers in the law-making process in the United Kingdom; the Executive overlaps with, and is part of, the Legislature (and, as we shall see, the judiciary, which currently also overlaps with both the Executive and the Legislature). Given the control that the Executive is normally able to exert over Parliament, the legislative function is, in practice, often dominated by the Executive.

Legislation enacted by the UK Parliament is known as a 'statute'. With the monarch's political role now reduced in practical terms to a cosmetic one, UK legislation represents the will of the highest law-making power in the United Kingdom. This notion stems from the fact that, in constitutional terms, the United Kingdom can be characterised as a 'parliamentary democracy'. This means that, except in particular spheres where it has voluntarily conceded power (e.g., on matters governed by the European Union, and those devolved to the Scottish Parliament, the Welsh Senned, and the Northern Ireland Assembly), the UK Parliament, as the supreme legislative body in the United Kingdom, is in theoretical terms empowered to enact any legal provisions whatsoever.

While in the interests of political expediency, Parliament may in practice try to refrain from enacting unpopular legislation, unlike legislative bodies in other countries (e.g., Canada, the United States and France), the UK Parliament is not required to act in accordance with some higher authority, such as a written constitution. Thus, primary legislation of the UK Parliament cannot be challenged in, nor overturned by, the courts of the land (although the Human Rights Act 1998, discussed below, provides and has provided a challenge to law makers in this sense).

## Scottish Acts

After the Act of Union 1707 established the new Westminster Parliament, Scotland was, in general, entitled to retain its own distinct laws and legal system (subject to the proviso that these could be overturned and amended by Acts of the Westminster Parliament).

The old Scottish Parliament was politically a largely primitive (and undemocratic) affair with little long-lasting influence. Most Acts of the old Scottish Parliament were repealed by subsequent UK legislation because of changing social norms and lack of modern relevance. They have fallen into *desuetude* (disuse) and are no longer considered enforceable. Since the Union of the Parliaments, all UK legislation has applied to Scotland unless the contrary is expressly stated.

Owing to pressures on parliamentary time and, perhaps, lack of interest, it has been common for UK-wide Acts of Parliament to include additional, bolted-on sections, which apply only to Scotland, with a view to preserving the different legal doctrines and rules that exist north of the border. Heavy criticism has been levelled against this practice (colloquially known as 'putting a kilt' on an Act) because it has failed to preserve the uniqueness of Scots law by largely ignoring its nuances and importing, wholesale, English legal principles. A contrary argument might be that, in the interests of efficiency and certainty, there is much to be said for harmonising spheres of law (such as that relating to commercial matters) across the whole of the United Kingdom – readers will come to their own conclusions as they encounter examples of this practice in different areas. A pertinent example is the (original) Sale of Goods Act 1893, which imported several English common law principles into Scots law. Its later incarnation, the Sale of Goods Act 1979, again applicable throughout the whole of the United Kingdom, has now been replaced by the Consumer Rights Act 2015.

It is worth noting that certain UK Parliament Acts apply *only* to Scotland. This is denoted by the word 'Scotland' appearing in brackets towards the end of the title of the Act – for example, the Bankruptcy (Scotland) Act 1985. However, the scope for Scotland-only Acts of the UK Parliament have been greatly reduced by the advent of the Scottish

Parliament, which has the devolved right to legislate for Scotland in several areas.

## Types of Act

There are several different types Act of the UK Parliament, including General Acts, Local Acts and Personal Acts:

- **General Acts** are the most important as these apply to the whole community (e.g., the Consumer Rights Act 2015).

- **Local Acts**, as the name suggests, are those which are restricted to a locality. They are quite uncommon, as most local legislative provisions are enacted by local authorities through the issuance of byelaws (see below).

- **Personal Acts** are relevant only to a person or group of persons. Many early Personal Acts pertained to the powers of the monarchy. There have been no Personal Acts since 1987.

## Public Bills

An Act's antecedent or origin is known as a 'Bill'. All General Acts begin as Public Bills. The bulk of Public Bills are brought to Parliament by the government in its role as the Executive. Hence, such Bills are generally promoted by the government minister responsible for the policy area (or 'portfolio') to which the proposed legislation pertains.

## Private Members' Bills

Some Public Bills, however, are brought forward by Members of Parliament (MPs) who are not members of the government. These MPs are granted the opportunity to bring forward their own proposals by means of a parliamentary ballot – these proposals are known as 'Private Members' Bills'. Given the fact that government has a tight timetable within which to enact its wide-ranging, intended statutory provisions, very few of these Bills become Acts. The tight timescales for their enactment mean that they are very easily 'talked out' by opponents and, in practice, Private Members' Bills normally require government support to succeed.

## Private Bills

Local and Personal Acts are brought as Private Bills. The reader should not confuse Private Bills with Private Members' Bills (which, as noted above, are in fact Public Bills). A Private Bill seeks the enactment of a piece of legislation that gives powers or benefits to a group of persons, such as a local council or private corporation. Such Bills are brought by the party seeking the requisite powers, petitioning Parliament in a process which is like a court hearing. The Bills are normally referred to a panel of MPs where those seeking such powers may put forward their case and those who may be adversely affected by such provision may lodge complaints.

An example of a Local Act is the Ipswich Market Act 2004, which regulates traffic use when there are local markets taking place. Another recent Private Bill that was successful and became a Local Act is the New Southgate Cemetery Act 2017. The Act gave over to New Southgate Cemetery and Crematorium Limited and the National Spiritual Assembly of the Bahá'is of the United Kingdom the ability 'to extinguish rights of burial and disturb human remains in respect of New Southgate Cemetery for the purpose of increasing the space for interments; and for connected purposes'.

Alternatively, examples of Personal Acts that commenced as Private Bills are the John Ernest Rolfe and Florence Iveen Rolfe (Marriage Enabling) Act and the George Donald Evans and Deborah Jane Evans (Marriage Enabling) Act, both passed in 1987. The Marriage Enabling Act 1960 authorises a person to marry certain kin of a former spouse.

## Hybrid Bills

Bills that exhibit features of both Public and Private Bills – being those primarily of relevance to a group of persons but which may impact upon the public in general – are termed 'hybrid' Bills. Hybrid bills are subject to Parliamentary procedures that relate to both Public and Private Bills. A good example of a hybrid Bill was the Crossrail Act, which received Royal Assent on 22 July 2008. If you reflect on the features of a hybrid Bill, you should be able to understand why this is. Crossrail is a new seventy-three-mile railway line crossing London from west to east that will better connect to the south east of the United Kingdom. In general, it affects everyone in the United Kingdom, but it has a specific impact on those living and working around its route.

## Rationale behind Acts of Parliament

The fundamental purpose of any Act of Parliament is to follow through on some policy initiative and bring about new law. Some Acts, however, do have technical purposes that denote a classification. Codifying Acts, for example, can be considered 'tidy up' exercises, designed to assimilate all existing common law and perhaps other statutes in each area and then frame it within a single piece of legislation. A prime example of a codifying Act is the original Sale of Goods Act 1893, which brought together the previous common law and statutory provisions.

In a similar vein, sometimes the purpose of legislation is to bring together existing Acts of Parliament that presently govern an area of law. In general, the purpose of these provisions is to render the law clearer and more accessible. Such legal enactments are termed 'Consolidation Acts'. A pertinent example of a Consolidation Act is the Health and Safety at Work Act 1974, that drew together important strands of several earlier provisions (including the Factories Act 1961, and the Offices, Shops and Railway Premises Act 1963) into one coherent place. Another is the Consumer Rights Act 2015. The Consumer Rights Act replaced three major pieces of consumer legislation: the Sale of Goods Act 1979; the Unfair Terms in Consumer Contracts Regulations 1999; and the Supply of Goods and Services Act 1982. The Consumer Rights Act was introduced to consider the modern digital age and simplify, strengthen and modernise the law, giving us clearer shopping rights.

A Declaratory Act is one that seeks to restate the law. This might be deemed necessary by government particularly in the aftermath of a controversial, unpopular or inconvenient court decision. One striking example of a Declaratory Act is the War Damage Act 1965, which was enacted following a House of Lords' decision (sitting as a court) that compelled the government to pay out compensation for its necessary destruction of British-owned company oil fields in 1942 during the Second World War (*Burmah Oil Co. (Burma Trading) Ltd* v *Lord Advocate* (1964)). This was to stop them falling into the hands of the advancing Japanese army. In *Burmah Oil Co.* the House of Lords agreed that the destruction was necessary due to the war situation, but also that compensation was owed to the Burmah Oil Company for its loss. To avoid subsequent and similar claims by others, the War Damages Act 1965 was passed. This Act is a rare example of the enactment of what can be termed as 'retrospective' legislation by the state, which, in this instance, nullified the hitherto valid claims of *other* oil-field owners for compensation. Legislating in such a retrospective fashion may at times entail human rights concerns (see the discussion on human rights below).

Statute Law Revision Acts are designed to repeal existing legislation that has become obsolete or is no longer of relevance in modern society. A Law Reform (Miscellaneous Provisions) Act is a common, and arguably unsatisfactory, method by which minor amendments can simultaneously be made to various areas of law. The lack of focus of such Acts may lead to poor legislation. Legislative provisions that have the aim of amending or updating a previous piece of legislation are known as Amendment

Acts. For instance, the Race Relations (Amendment) Act 2000 brought about particular reforms of the earlier Race Relations Act 1976. If any ambiguity exists between the provisions of the original legislation and those of the amendment Act, the provisions of the latter will be enforced as they represent the latest expression of the will of Parliament.

## THE LEGISLATIVE PROCESS FOR PUBLIC BILLS

Here we focus on the law-making process for Public Bills – being the most important kind of legislation passed by the Westminster Parliament. Acts of the Westminster Parliament are subject to a somewhat convoluted, and often lengthy, legislative journey.

### Pre-parliamentary procedures

It is important to note that pre-parliamentary processes have a major impact on the composition of any new Bill – a 'Bill' being the origin of any Act that ultimately becomes law.

The life of any Public Bill (except for Private Members' Bills) begins with the government considering what policy measures it wishes to put to Parliament. These often originate in the majority party's election manifesto. At this early stage, government may be influenced by several factors and advice may be obtained, and consultation sought, from internal and external bodies. Advice may be sought, and representation obtained, from government departmental and inter-departmental committees. With regard to particularly technical areas of law (often termed 'lawyers' law') – such as company, partnership and insolvency law – law reform bodies such as the Law Commission of England and Wales and the Scottish Law Commission may be called upon for input. Independent pressure and interest groups may also seek to influence the policy-making process.

An example of a pressure group would be Greenpeace, with its environmental concerns; while an example of an interest group would be the Automobile Association (known as 'the AA'), which represent the interests of UK drivers. Over recent years, these cultural and occupational groupings have gained importance as players in the political game. They campaign in a variety of policy areas including animal welfare, education, the environment, equality for ethnic minorities, health, housing, rural affairs and welfare rights. Some interest and pressure groups have more political clout than others and, similarly, their methods of gaining influence on policy vary widely from petitioning government and writing to MPs, to urban terrorism and violent protests.

Consultation also takes place in the public eye. Governments may publish initial Green Papers setting out broad policy ideas and inviting representations thereon from the public. Similarly, White Papers, which entail more defined expressions of legislative intent, may also be published. It should be noted, however, that the government is not required to issue either Green or White Papers prior to publishing a Bill. Public consultation does not normally allow the public to vote on any proposed provision.

In respect of measures of legislative importance, however, a public referendum *may* be called. Two of note in recent years are the Scottish Independence Referendum 2014 – a proposal rejected by the Scottish electorate 55.3 per cent to 44.7 per cent – and the EU Referendum 2016 – which saw the UK electorate narrowly vote to leave the European Union at 51.9 per cent to 48.1 per cent.

When the consultation period has ended, a Bill will be presented to Parliament. The drafting of the Bill is generally undertaken by highly skilled 'Parliamentary Counsel' (special legal draftsmen) on the advice of the government department concerned. The drafting process can be long and arduous. Poor drafting may lead to later problems with the interpretation of statutes (discussed below) and can provide loopholes in the law for lawyers to later exploit. In the name of open government, and perhaps to alleviate difficulties with interpretation, in 1997 the then Labour government announced its intention to publish an increased number of 'draft Bills'.

## Stages of the parliamentary process

A Bill may be introduced in *either* of the two parliamentary chambers: the House of Commons; or the House of Lords. Given that the bulk of legislation arises from the Executive (government), most Acts originate in the House of Commons. Indeed, certain provisions (e.g., those relating to tax and finance) must *always* be introduced in the House of Commons.

### The Commons

The House of Commons – historically the lower-status House, but now at the heart of the legislative process – comprises 650 MPs, including fifty-nine Scottish MPs. MPs are elected on a one-per-constituency, first-past-the-post basis, under the Fixed-term Parliaments Act 2011, for a five-year period. It is, however, likely that as a result of the 12 December 2019 General Election that saw the Conservative Party return to government with an overall majority of eighty, the United Kingdom's new Conservative prime minister will at some point in the next few years bring a proposal to Parliament to abolish the Fixed-term Parliaments Act, fulfilling one of the 2019 Manifesto commitments in so doing ('Get Brexit Done', *The Conservative and Unionist Party 2019 Manifesto*, p. 48).

## The Lords

Alternatively, the 'Upper House' or House of Lords comprises four different sorts of member or 'peers' – namely, 677 or so 'life peers' (life-long members appointed by the Crown, who are, in practice, appointed on the advice of the prime minister, although the process for appointment has become more transparent of late); twenty-six Anglican archbishops and senior diocesan bishops of the Church of England; and eighty-eight hereditary peers who hold a historic birthright to sit in the House. Most hereditary peerages were abolished by the House of Lords Act 1999, and the eighty-eight hereditary peers is the residual number of what remains of the 700 hereditary peers that hitherto dominated the House of Lords. Whether hereditary peers should remain part of the United Kingdom's legislature is a matter of continuing political debate.

## Reform of the House of Lords

Reform of the House of Lords has been discussed since 1886 when the Commons debated whether there should be a hereditary right to sit in the Lords. Ever since then, proposed reform of the House of Lords has been fraught with difficulty. The latest being in 2007 when the Labour government under Prime Minister Gordon Brown published its White Paper, 'The House of Lords: Reform', setting out the policy for a hybrid House of Lords with 50 per cent elected members and 50 per cent appointed members.

In March 2007, the House of Commons voted on the options for composition supporting an elected House of Lords. A week later the House of Lords voted on composition favouring a fully-appointed House. This later led to the next government – a Conservative-Liberal Democrat coalition – introducing the House of Lords Reform Bill in May 2012, which in August of that year was abruptly dropped. Thus, while there seems to be a general appetite for retention of some form of second chamber within Parliament – primarily to act as a brake and monitor the otherwise oft-untrammelled power of government – any clear view on the future constitution and powers of the House of Lords remains elusive. (For a recent update on the state of reform of the House of Lords, see: www. parliament.uk/business/lords/lords-history/lords-reform/)

## Procedure in Parliament

How a Bill becomes an Act:

- **First reading** – the Bill is normally presented at first reading. This is a formal exercise where MPs are informed about the proposed legislation and a date is announced for the second reading of the Bill.

- **Second reading** – the first parliamentary debate on the Bill, where a discussion of the Bill's main policy themes will take place with government ministers and their opposition 'shadow' equivalents both making opening and closing speeches. A vote will then take place as to whether the Bill should proceed.

- **Committee stage** – if it is to proceed, the Bill is then examined by a parliamentary committee comprising MPs reflecting the balance of political power in the House in which the Bill originated. The committee then analyses the detail of the Bill in a comprehensive scrutinising process. If the Bill is of significance, the committee can comprise all MPs and thus the scrutiny here is undertaken by a *Committee of the Whole House.*

- **Report stage** – upon completion of its analysis, the committee reports back to the House, often with several proposed amendments. These amendments may be discussed and voted on in the House. Moreover, new amendments may be lodged at this time.

- **Third reading** – a third reading may take place immediately after the report stage. The Bill is read a final time, which in effect amounts to a motion that it be passed.

If the Bill completes its journey in the Commons, it will then be considered in much the same way by the House of Lords. It should be noted that presently the Lords can, in general, only delay an Act for one year. By using the Parliament Act 1949, the House of Commons can ultimately force through any legislation without the consent of the Lords. Such a move is considered politically controversial, however, and has occurred on only a handful of occasions since the 1949 Act was passed – the most recent being the Lords' frustration of the controversial Hunting Act 2004, which banned the hunting of foxes with dogs.

At the end of the parliamentary process, the Bill must be forwarded to the monarch for *Royal Assent* before it can become law. By constitutional convention (a customary rule of the constitution), however, the monarch would never refuse to give such consent. If the monarch disapproves of any proposed Act, he or she may comment on this in private. In what may be an apocryphal tale, when, in the late nineteenth century, Parliament sought to make both male homosexuality and lesbianism a crime, Queen Victoria viewed the criminalisation of lesbianism inappropriate on the basis that she could not contemplate that it existed.

An Act that has become law will often come into force (or 'commence') whenever Royal Assent is given. However, in order to allow affected parties to make preparation for any new law, as is often the case, an Act will commence at a later date – either with reference to a time frame in the Act itself or where a provision empowers a government minister or some other person to set a date for commencement.

## Legislation of the Scottish Parliament

At the time of writing, the Scottish Parliament is in its fifth parliamentary session. Many Acts of the Scottish Parliament have been passed since its inception with the Scotland Act 1998. Its first – the Mental Health (Public Safety and Appeals) (Scotland) Act 1999 – closed a loophole in the law which led to the release of mentally ill killer Noel Ruddle from the state hospital at Carstairs after successfully arguing that the hospital's treatment programmes were no longer of benefit to him (see below).

Of interest from the Scottish Parliament's second session (2003–7) is the Tenements (Scotland) Act 2004, which is now the main source of the law of the tenement regulating tenement flats in Scotland. The Judiciary and Courts (Scotland) Act 2008, passed during its third session (2007–11), set out reforms to the courts of Scotland to give statutory force to its judicial independence and to establish the Lord President of the Court of Session as Head of the Judiciary of Scotland. More recently, in its fourth session (2011–16), Parliament enacted seventy-nine Acts, including the Alcohol (Minimum Pricing) (Scotland) Act 2012, and the Forth Road Bridge Act 2013. In its fifth session (2016–) a number of important Acts have been passed, including the Air Departure Tax (Scotland) Act 2017, and the repeal of the controversial Offensive Behaviour at Football and Threatening Communications Act 2011 in 2018.

## COMPOSITION OF THE SCOTTISH PARLIAMENT

The Scottish Parliament is *unicameral*, meaning there is only one legislative chamber. The Parliament comprises 129 Members of the Scottish Parliament (MSPs). Of this cohort, seventy-three are elected on a first-past-the-post, *constituency* basis, while a further fifty-six are appointed from *regional lists* using a proportional representation procedure known as the 'additional member system'.

The Executive or Scottish Government in Scotland's devolved law-making arrangement is composed of a first minister and several other ministers, who are also MSPs. Hence, again, as is the case at Westminster, there is no strict separation of powers between the executive and legislative functions of government.

## DEVOLUTION AND THE SCOTLAND ACT

The Scottish Parliament's legislative powers are *devolved*, which means that they have arisen from powers handed down by the Westminster Parliament via the Scotland Act 1998. This fact is important in that the Scottish Parliament's powers can therefore generally be considered as subordinate to the authority of the UK Parliament; a situation that arises constitutionally.

The Scotland Act 1998 empowered the new Parliament to enact law in all policy matters pertaining to Scotland, save particular 'reserved' areas, which remain the exclusive preserve of the UK Parliament. These reserved matters include UK constitutional issues; foreign affairs; defence; fiscal and economic policy (although the Scottish Parliament has limited tax-raising powers); most social security; and employment. Under s. 29(1) of the Scotland Act, the Scottish Parliament cannot encroach upon any reserved matter. Because of promises made by leaders and former leaders of the major political parties at Westminster during the Scottish independence campaign of 2014, powers to the Scottish Parliament were enhanced under the Scotland Act 2016, as was its status. Its Part 1 amended the 1998 Scotland Act with a new s. 63(A), now emphasising the *permanency* of the Scottish Parliament. Holyrood – where the Scottish Parliament sits in Edinburgh – can now legislate on new areas such as personal income tax, equal opportunities, consumer advocacy and advice, abortion law, speed limits and gaming machines. Further, additional new powers on welfare have also been devolved and are due to be transferred later. Despite the wide range of reserved matters, the policy areas that remain do, nevertheless, represent a significant opportunity for Parliament to enact legislation. It should be noted, however, that, given the constitutional supremacy of the UK Parliament, even in respect of devolved areas, the UK Parliament could continue to legislate for Scotland (as is expressly provided for in s. 28(7) of the Scotland Act 1998). It would be somewhat unsatisfactory, however, if, after setting up the new Scottish body, the Westminster Parliament continually rode roughshod over its devolved powers when it deemed fit to do so.

## The Sewel Convention

Thus, in what can be considered a very British solution (because an agreement is made by a non-legal convention rather than by strict legal means), such points of tension between Holyrood and Westminster are addressed by what are referred to as *'legislative consent motions'*, otherwise known as the 'Sewel Convention' (named after Lord Sewel), by virtue of which, under s. 28 of the Scotland Act 1998, the Westminster Parliament would only encroach on devolved areas with the consent of Scottish Parliament, through what are termed 'Sewel motions'.

Sewel motions themselves have become an issue of controversy.

## Legislative consent motions

It was originally intended that Sewel motions would be used only on rare occasions where it was deemed more convenient for Westminster to legislate across the United Kingdom. An example of successful legislation passed via a Sewel motion that exemplifies such is the Civil Partnership Act 2004. Another example is Legislative Consent Motion S5M-21322 struck between Holyrood and Westminster in March 2020, agreeing that the relevant provisions of the Coronavirus Bill (later Act), introduced in the House of Commons, 'so far as it fell within the legislative competence of the Scottish Parliament or altered the executive competence of Scottish Ministers, should be considered by the UK Parliament'.

A more controversial use of the Sewel Convention occurred in 2018 when the Scottish Parliament passed its UK Withdrawal from the European Union (Legal Continuity) (Scotland) Bill that challenged the Westminster Government's European Union (Withdrawal) Act 2018 regarding what was to happen post-EU withdrawal to legislative powers when repatriated back from the European Union to the United Kingdom after the transition period ending 31 December 2020. The Scottish Parliament wanted powers in already devolved areas given to Holyrood immediately on transfer – hence, its European Union (Legal Continuity) (Scotland) Bill. The Westminster Parliament disagreed. This led to accusations by the Scottish Parliament of a 'power grab' by Westminster and saw a reference by the Attorney General and the Advocate General for Scotland to the Supreme Court of the United Kingdom regarding the veracity of the European Union (Withdrawal) Act, questioning Westminster's sovereign ability to hold onto repatriated powers that until Brexit had largely been governed by EU law. The Supreme Court, however, pronounced Holyrood's Legal Continuity Bill legislatively incompetent and thus 'not law'.

## THE LEGISLATIVE PROCESS IN THE SCOTTISH PARLIAMENT

The law-making processes of the Scottish Parliament differ somewhat from those of its UK counterpart. The Scotland Act 1998 makes scant provision concerning legislative procedures, save that by virtue of s. 22 the Parliament must adopt Standing Orders to ensure that any Bill proposed is subject to three readings prior to adoption (Standing Orders of the Scottish Parliament, Edition 4 (11 November 2011)). (While a summary is provided below; for an excellent detailed review of Scottish parliamentary procedures, see: www.parliament.scot/visitandlearn/100529.aspx)

The Scottish Parliament must take care that it passes only those laws it is competent to pass. In this sense, several safeguards are built into its law-making procedures. First, when a Bill is brought to Parliament it must be accompanied by a written statement from the Presiding Officer outlining his or her view on whether the proposed Act falls within the scope of the Parliament's devolved powers. The Presiding Officer is an MSP but is politically impartial. The role of the Presiding Officer is, generally, to chair parliamentary meetings and ensure that the legislative process runs in an appropriate and lawful manner.

Akin to the legislative process at Westminster, most Bills are the product of executive action. Bills may on occasion be brought by individual MSPs (termed 'Members' Bills'). Where the Bill is brought by the Scottish Government (known as an 'Executive Bill'), it must also be accompanied by a written statement from the appropriate minister affirming that the legislative proposals fall within the scope of the Parliament's competence.

In addition, the Bill should be accompanied by:

- a policy memorandum outlining the policy objectives of the legislation;
- a statement of any consultation which has preceded the Bill;
- explanatory notes summarising the Bill's contents;
- a statement of consideration of alternative policy approaches; and
- an assessment of the Bill's impact on a variety of factors including equal opportunities, human rights, sustainable development and island communities.

### Enactment of legislation at Holyrood

The parliamentary process for Bills in the Scottish Parliament varies according to the *type* of Bill being proposed. The following represents the most common procedure:

- **Stage 1** – the Bill is first forwarded to a committee dealing with the relevant area of policy to which the Bill relates (known as the 'lead committee'). The committee then considers the general principles of the Bill and reports back to Parliament. The general scope and provisions of the Bill are then considered by Parliament in the light of the committee's report. It is possible at this stage for the Bill to be referred back to the lead committee for a further report on any aspect of it before Parliament makes its decision.

- **Stage 2** – if Parliament has agreed upon the general principles of the Bill, it is then sent back to the lead committee, or alternatively to a committee of the whole Parliament (and in some cases both), where the Bill's provisions are scrutinised and amendments can be proposed.

- **Stage 3** – the amended Bill is then considered by the Parliament as a whole and a vote is taken to decide whether the Bill will be passed. Additional amendments may be lodged at this point.

If the Bill is passed by the Parliament, the Presiding Officer is duty bound to then forward it to the monarch for Royal Assent. Prior to this occurring, however, and within four weeks of the passing of the Bill, by virtue of s. 33 of the Scotland Act 1998, a number of personnel (namely, the Advocate General, the Attorney General or the Lord Advocate) can refer the Bill to the UK Supreme Court for it to examine whether it falls within the legislative scope of the Scottish Parliament. (Scotland's legal personnel are discussed in more detail in Chapter 5; the Supreme Court is discussed in Chapter 3.) Note, the Constitutional Reform Act 2005 – creating a Supreme Court in the United Kingdom – commenced operation in October 2009 and abolished the appellate jurisdiction of the House of Lords (sitting as a court). Under the new arrangements the Privy Council functions are also subsumed within the new Supreme Court. As a further monitor on the Scottish Parliament's legislative powers, under s. 35 of the Scotland Act 1998, the Secretary of State for Scotland (a member of government at Westminster) may issue an order forbidding the Presiding Officer from forwarding the Bill for Royal Assent.

The general prohibitions on law making for the Scottish Parliament are set out in s. 29 and include provision that the Scottish Parliament may not legislate in respect of reserved matters; make laws contrary to European Community law or the European Convention on Human Rights and Fundamental Freedoms; legislate for another country or territory; or legislate contrary to certain specified Westminster statutes including the Human Rights Act 1998, the Scotland Act 1998, the Scotland Act 2016 and the Act of Union 1707.

## THE GROWTH OF NATIONALISM

In the fourth election to the Scottish Parliament in 2011, the pro-independence SNP achieved what was thought electorally impossible. Despite Scotland's more representative dual voting system – first-past-the-post and the additional member system – the SNP achieved an *overall* majority at Holyrood, winning sixty-nine seats (Labour thirty-seven seats; Conservative fifteen seats; Liberal Democrats five seats; Scottish Greens two seats; and, completing the 129 available seats, one independent MSP). Realising its opportunity, and in fulfilment of a manifesto promise, the newly elected 2011 SNP government then prepared to ask the Scottish people to back independence and secede from the rest of the United Kingdom.

### The Edinburgh Agreement

The first step towards holding a Scottish Independence Referendum was the Edinburgh Agreement signed on 15 October 2012 at St Andrew's House, Edinburgh. This '*Agreement between the United Kingdom Government and the Scottish Government on a Referendum on Independence for Scotland*'[1] laid down the terms under which the 2014 referendum would be held. Both governments agreed that the referendum should:

- have a clear legal base;
- be legislated for by the Scottish Parliament;
- be conducted to command the confidence of parliaments, government and people; and
- deliver a fair test and decisive expression of the views of people in Scotland and a result that everyone will respect.

The governments agreed to promote an Order in Council under s. 30 of the Scotland Act 1998 to allow a single-question referendum on Scottish independence to be held before the end of 2014, to be legislated for and administered by the Scottish Parliament itself. The agreement was signed by Prime Minister David Cameron, Secretary of State for Scotland Michael Moore, First Minister Alex Salmond and Deputy First Minister Nicola Sturgeon. Then followed the passing of the Scottish

---

[1] The Agreement between the UK Government and the Scottish Government on a Referendum on Independence for Scotland, <https://assets.publishing.service.gov.uk/government/uploads/system/uploads/attachment_data/file/313612/scottish_referendum_agreement.pdf>.

Independence Referendum Act 2013 and the Scottish Independence Referendum (Franchise) Act 2013 at Holyrood, both of which enabled the subsequent Scottish Independence Referendum 2014.

## Scottish Independence Referendum 2014

Following a two-year campaign, the following question was put to the Scottish people on 18 September 2014: 'Should Scotland be an independent country?'. Of the Scottish electorate, 84.6 per cent went to the polls; 44.7 per cent or 1,617,989 voted 'yes' in favour; and 55.3 per cent or 2,001,926 voted 'no' against.

SNP First Minister Alex Salmond immediately demitted office and his deputy Nicola Sturgeon was elected unopposed as leader of the SNP, and by dint of position and her party's Parliamentary majority, became the fourth, and current, First Minister of Scotland.

## DELEGATED LEGISLATION OF THE UK PARLIAMENT

The dynamism of our times has seen a rising need for the enactment of more and more legislation in a multitude of different policy areas. With the lengthy and complex UK legislative process and its time constraints, it is not possible to enact primary legislation in terms of statutes to meet all perceived policy need. Statutory provisions, therefore, do not always originate directly from primary legislation, but rather enter into force by another route in what can be termed 'delegated legislation' (or 'secondary legislation'). Delegated legislation encompasses situations where the right to legislate has been delegated by Parliament to some other person or entity. There are two main types of delegated legislation: statutory instruments (or regulations); and byelaws.

### Statutory instruments

Under powers bestowed by an *enabling* (or parent) Act of Parliament (a pertinent example being the Health and Safety at Work Act 1974), government ministers may be subsequently empowered or *vested* with the right to formulate their own statutory instruments within the ambit of an Act. Ministers are also given latitude by way of primary and secondary legislation to take policy decisions within their ministerial portfolio. For example, the home secretary is empowered to take decisions pertaining to individual immigration and citizenship cases.

The Act of Parliament empowering ministers to enact delegated legislation may itself merely prescribe a general policy framework which must be implemented in practice by the minister concerned through delegated legislation and policy decisions. Under the Statutory Instruments Act 1946, such ministerial legislative measures are termed 'statutory instruments'.

## Orders in Council and the Royal Prerogative

Government ministers may also issue 'Orders in Council', made in pursuance of what can be termed the 'Royal Prerogative'. The Royal Prerogative relates to several residual powers of the monarch that the government can now implement by virtue of its modern constitutional status as 'the Queen in Parliament'. Such orders are enacted when the Queen's representatives in the Privy Council rubber-stamp draft orders presented to them by government. Unfettered prerogative powers are an oddity in modern society and their continued existence in modern times could be considered an affront to democracy. Nevertheless, some important powers are vested in government through the Royal Prerogative, including the right to declare war and the right to enter treaties with other nations.

In other cases, the right to make Orders in Council in specified situations does not arise constitutionally but has been expressly conferred upon the Crown (and hence government) through Acts of Parliament. For example, the Emergency Powers (Defence) Act 1939 empowered the Crown (and, in practice, therefore the government) to make Orders in Council to ensure public safety after an outbreak of war.

## Byelaws

Much law enacted is of a local nature, affecting only particular local communities. In this sense, local authorities (e.g., Glasgow City Council or Edinburgh City Council) are empowered to enact 'byelaws' which apply to their geographical areas of governance, primarily by the Local Government (Scotland) Act 1973 (as amended).

The enactment of byelaws allows Scotland's thirty-two local authorities to undertake several regulatory functions and tackle local nuisances and associated community problems. Byelaws may be and have been passed in different areas, including the regulation of alcohol consumption; the licensing of betting shops, saunas and tattoo parlours; the prohibition of ball games in public places; and the prohibition of fishing in certain rivers. Importantly, byelaws do not normally come into force until they are confirmed by some governmental authority (generally a government minister).

# DELEGATED LEGISLATION CREATED BY THE SCOTTISH COURTS

It may seem unconstitutional for courts to be granted the power to enact laws. However, Acts of Parliament do vest or empower the Scottish courts to prescribe new rules for court procedure. Thus, an *'Act of Sederunt'* is a rule formulated by the Court of Session under delegated powers under s. 16 of the Administration of Justice (Scotland) Act 1933. This Act allows the Court of Session to alter its own procedure or that in the Sheriff Courts. Other primary Acts of Parliament also allow the Court of Session to enact Acts of Sederunt, such as the Sheriff Courts (Scotland) Act 1971.

Similarly, under the Criminal Procedure (Scotland) Act 1975, the High Court of Justiciary may pass *'Acts of Adjournal'* to bring about reform of criminal court procedure.

## Sub-delegated legislation

Sub-delegated legislation, whereby the party empowered to enact delegation by Parliament passes that right to do so onto another, is rare. Most parent Acts of Parliament allow for one level of delegation only; indeed, there is a presumption that Parliament intends sub-delegation not to take place. This presumption has its origins in the well-established common law rule of agency that declares an agent (or delegate) acting on behalf of someone cannot themselves delegate to someone else.

Notwithstanding, from time to time sub-delegation does take place. An oft-cited example of sub-delegated legislation arose at the time of the Second World War with the enactment of the Emergency Powers (Defence) Act 1939. The Act enabled ministers to make orders which provided authority for others to make directions which, in turn, allowed others to issue certain licences in specified circumstances.

## Delegated legislation: checks and balances

There are a few ways in which the exercise of delegated legislation can be monitored. Its principal control stems from its *enabling* Act of Parliament, which sets out the legislative framework or area of discretion within which subsequent delegated legislation can be crafted. Monitoring may also take place within and outwith Parliament.

Internal monitoring within Parliament takes place initially under ss. 4–7 of the Statutory Instruments Act 1946. As such, any ministerial statutory instruments must be 'laid' before either House of Parliament. MPs are then able to scrutinise the instrument for a three-week period prior to it entering into force. While this does not provide any real check on ministerial discretion, one of two further parliamentary monitoring procedures will normally be applied, known as the 'negative' resolution procedure and 'affirmative' resolution procedure.

## Negative resolution procedure

Use of the negative resolution procedure is the most common. Following s. 16 of the Legislative and Regulatory Reform Act 2006, a statutory instrument (or SI) laid under the negative procedure becomes law on the day that the minister signs it, and automatically remains law unless a motion – or 'prayer' – to reject it is agreed by either House within forty sitting days.

## Affirmative resolution procedure

Less common is the affirmative resolution procedure as set out in s. 17 of the Legislative and Regulatory Reform Act 2006. In these instances, the statutory instrument will not come into force until it is actively approved by a vote in both Houses of Parliament.

It has been argued that considering the government's dominant role in Parliament, statutory instruments are rarely nullified in these ways.

## Further scrutiny of delegated legislation

More direct control is exercised over delegated legislation when statutory instruments are scrutinised by Parliament's Joint Committee on Statutory Instruments comprising members from both chambers. The committee can refer the delegated legislation back to either House on any of eight specified grounds, as well as on a 'catch-all' discretionary basis.

A further check on delegated legislation can occur by way of a petition brought before the Court of Session by an affected party who has sufficient 'standing' to bring such an action. Standing, or *locus standi*, demands the petitioner has sufficient interest in the matter to which the petition relates. The Court of Session may then grant the petition and overturn any exercise of delegated legislation under a process termed 'judicial review'. If it appears that a particular statutory instrument is beyond the powers of its enabling Act – which may include circumstances in which it is subject to some procedural irregularity – has been enacted by the wrong person or body, is manifestly unreasonable or motivated by improper considerations, then the Court of Session may strike the instrument down as *ultra vires*. It should be noted that courts are, in general, not concerned with the merits of the legislation, but rather whether its enactment was legal under the various grounds above, or otherwise.

It is also important to reiterate here that given the doctrine of UK parliamentary supremacy, courts cannot strike down a primary Act of Parliament; but the judiciary can cast aside the exercise of delegated legislation, which in itself is not an expression of the will of Parliament.

## Delegated legislation of the Scottish Parliament

In one sense, all Acts of the Scottish Parliament amount to delegated legislation in that the Scottish Parliament's powers to enact legislation are devolved from the Scotland Act 1998, which is a piece of Westminster legislation. As noted in Chapter 2, prior to a Bill receiving Royal Assent there is a cooling off period during which it may be subject to review by the Supreme Court to ensure that it falls within the ambit of Parliament's powers. However, given that legislation of the Scottish Parliament is not constitutionally supreme, its legislation can be subject to judicial review even after it has been given Royal Assent. To some extent this gives courts a new, constitutional role. For the first time courts can take issue with Acts of Parliament, albeit those of the devolved Scottish Parliament. None of the above, however, detracts from the general principle of Westminster parliamentary supremacy.

## CHALLENGES TO SCOTTISH LEGISLATION

A good example of a challenge to legislation of the Scottish Parliament can be found in the high-profile case of Noel Ruddle, mentioned earlier in this chapter. Noel Ruddle was a psychopath who had been sent to be detained indefinitely in a secure mental institution in 1991 after he had killed his neighbour with a Kalashnikov rifle. However, because of a loophole in mental health legislation, and amidst a howl of protests, he was released in 1999. Several other individuals concurrently incarcerated in secure mental institutions and in a similar position to Ruddle, subsequently sought their release too. In response, the Scottish Executive, as it was then known, closed this *lacuna* in the law with the enactment of the Mental Health (Scotland) Act 1999.

To avoid a flurry of similar cases this law was made retrospective. This nullified the rights of action of other parties also seeking release on the same basis. Consequently, it was challenged in the Court of Session on the basis that the retrospective nature of the legislation, which defeated what might otherwise be a valid claim in law, was contrary to the Parliament's human rights obligations. We should perhaps be thankful that the claim was unsuccessful; the new Act stood and Ruddle's contemporaries remained incarcerated (see *A* v *Scottish Ministers* (2001)).

## Scottish statutory instruments

The Scottish Parliament, like Westminster, may delegate powers to its ministers and others. Again, any ministerial instruments must be laid before the Holyrood Parliament. These Scottish statutory instruments (SSIs) are then referred to a committee of the Scottish Parliament within whose remit the legislation falls (the 'lead committee'), or the special Subordinate Legislation Committee. The role of these committees is generally threefold to ensure that the instrument:

• is not *ultra vires* or outwith the powers set out in its enabling Act;
• is properly drafted; and
• does not encroach upon any reserved matter at Westminster.

Any adverse issues can then be debated in the Scottish Parliament. Like Westminster, Scottish statutory instruments are subject to one of two Scottish parliament procedural checks.

## Affirmative and negative Scottish statutory instruments

Affirmative instruments are normally laid before the Scottish Parliament in draft form and require the approval of the Parliament to enter into force. Negative instruments are usually made (i.e., signed by a minister) before they are laid before the Parliament. They typically come into force twenty-eight days after they are laid, unless there is a motion to the contrary.

Like primary Acts of the Scottish Parliament, delegated legislation is also reviewable in the Court of Session.

## Delegated legislation: advantages and disadvantages

Delegated legislation is clearly a necessity in any modern legal system. Its principle advantage is that it provides a solution to the vast amount of parliamentary time and resources that would be necessary to pass all required regulation solely by way of primary legislation. In contrast, delegated legislation can be enacted quickly. This may be important in meeting the requirements of novel contingencies, regulating new, hitherto unanticipated technologies, and reacting to shifting social *mores*. Delegated legislation is key in emergency situations where swift action is important, such as during wartime.

Finally, in particularly technical areas of policy, detailed legislation and policy decisions can be crafted by specialists in the field rather than by a largely ignorant Parliament. While delegated legislation is expedient, it may, however, be considered a 'necessary evil' in that it is democratically deficient. This is because parties other than elected MPs are empowered to take decisions which affect the public. Such concerns are exacerbated by the limited control which is exercised in practice over delegated legislation. These claims may be particularly pertinent in respect of the oft-extensive legislative clout wielded by government ministers. Of course, the UK Parliament does have some means of reining in the excesses of ministerial legislative power but, given the dearth of time and resources available to the monitoring committees, it has been seriously doubted whether they are practically of much effect.

The court process of judicial review is also somewhat unsatisfactory. The Court of Session is unable to intervene in legislative matters of its own volition. It can act only when a party petitions it for judicial review. However, the exorbitant costs involved in litigation of this sort, and the limited availability of legal aid, may militate against judicial review being sought through the courts. Even if an action is successful, a remedy is and can only be granted after the wrong has taken place. Moreover, in many instances, the court may find itself constricted by the fact that, as noted above, judicial review does not provide the opportunity for a challenge on the merits of any given ministerial action; in short, statutory instruments may be overturned only on the basis that they are outwith or *ultra vires* of the powers bestowed on the actor by the enabling Act.

The modern trend is for such parent Acts to vest wide discretionary legislative powers in ministers that provide scant scope for challenge. Moreover, clauses in enabling Acts may empower a minister to amend the terms of the Act itself through delegated legislation, which may effectively cut courts out of the loop. Such controversial provisions are often termed 'Henry VIII clauses'. However, the Human Rights Act 1998 has created a new battleground in which ministerial actions *can* be challenged in the courtroom (see, e.g., *Pretty* v *United Kingdom* (2002); *R* v *A* (2001) (complainant's sexual history); *R* v *Lambert (Steven)* (2001); *Re S (Children)* (2002) (care order: implementation of care plan), among others). The impact of the Human Rights Act is discussed further below.

## EUROPEAN UNION LAW

### Brexit

As noted in Chapter 1, law stemming from the European Union has become increasingly significant in the United Kingdom over recent years. So much so that cynics might say that it helped precipitate the United

Kingdom's exit from the European Union on 31 December 2020 following the EU Referendum in 2016.

## EU Referendum 2016

The road to Brexit probably began almost 50 years ago when, because of a manifesto commitment, the incoming Labour Government put Britain's continuing membership of the European Community to the people by way of a referendum – the first ever time that an issue had been decided *vox populi.*

Following the passing of the Referendum Act 1975, a referendum on European Community entry was held on the 5 June 1975. It attracted a 64 per cent turnout, with 67 per cent voting in favour of continued membership, and 33 per cent voting against. Tensions over EC membership never really went away, and pressure built, particularly within the Conservative Party, to put to the people the question of continued UK EU membership once again.

A referendum promise to this effect was therefore included in the Conservative Party manifesto for the May 2015 General Election – an election that they won. Prime Minister David Cameron then introduced the European Union Referendum Act 2015, which precipitated the 23 June 2016 EU Referendum. The question put was: '*Should the United Kingdom remain a member of the European Union or leave the European Union?*'. The electorate was asked to indicate whether the United Kingdom should '*Remain a member of the European Union*' or '*Leave the European Union*'. This saw UK voters vote narrowly to leave the European Union at 51.9 per cent to 48.1 per cent.

The day after the EU Referendum result on 24 June 2016, David Cameron announced his resignation with effect from the Conservative Party Conference in October 2016. A Conservative Party leadership contest ensued, which resulted in the election of Theresa May, who assumed the premiership. On taking office she declared that the United Kingdom would trigger Article 50 of the Treaty on European Union in early 2017.

## Article 50

Article 50 of the Treaty on European Union, enacted by the Treaty of Lisbon 2009, introduced a procedure for a Member State to withdraw voluntarily from the European Union. Of significance are Article 50(2) and Article 50(3). Article 50(2) states that:

> A Member State which decides to withdraw shall notify the European Council of its intention. In the light of the guidelines provided by the European Council, the Union shall negotiate and conclude

an agreement with that State, setting out the arrangements for its withdrawal, taking account of the framework for its future relationship with the Union.

Article 50(3) reads:

The Treaties shall cease to apply to the State in question from the date of entry into force of the withdrawal agreement or, failing that, two years after the notification referred to in paragraph 2, unless the European Council, in agreement with the Member State concerned, unanimously decides to extend this period.

Notification of withdrawal, by triggering Article 50, and then coming to an agreement concerning the United Kingdom's and European Union's future relationship – within the strict two-year time frame – was to prove both difficult and tumultuous.

### R (Miller) v Secretary of State for Exiting the EU 2016

Anticipating parliamentary turmoil in extricating the United Kingdom from the European Union, Prime Minister May initially favoured post-Article 50 withdrawal by way of ministerial delegated legislation. This saw rising opposition from those who saw Parliament and not the government as the United Kingdom's sovereign law-making body. The legislature and not the executive should oversee the process, finding cross-party favour in the House of Commons.

This was given impetus, as activist Gina Miller concurrently won an action in the English High Court against the government over its authority to implement Brexit without legislative approval from Parliament. The government then appealed to the Supreme Court. In *R (Miller)* v *Secretary of State for Exiting the European Union*, the Supreme Court – by a majority of 8:3 – upheld the earlier High Court ruling that the UK Government could not initiate withdrawal from the European Union by formal notification to the Council of the European Union as prescribed by Article 50 without an Act of Parliament permitting the government to do so.

### European Union (Notification of Withdrawal) Act 2017

As a result, in January 2017 in a government *volte face*, the Secretary of State for Exiting the European Union formally introduced a Bill that, on the 16 March 2017, was enacted without amendment as the European Union (Notification of Withdrawal) Act 2017. It provided both for repeal of the European Communities Act 1972, and for parliamentary

approval to be required for any subsequent withdrawal agreement negoti-
ated between HM Government and the European Union.

On 29 March 2017 Prime Minister Theresa May, in adherence to
Article 50, sent the President of the European Council Donald Tusk a
letter formally notifying the European Union of the United Kingdom's
intention to leave the European Union – and the clock began to tick on
the United Kingdom's exit from the EU.

## Brexit and the devolved administrations

An important subscript here is that in *R (Miller)* v *Secretary of State for Exiting the European Union* (2016) the case was *intervened* by the Lord Advocate on behalf of the Scottish Government; Counsel General on behalf of
the Welsh Senned; and applicants for judicial review in Northern Ireland.
These *intervenors* had their separate applications considered by the Supreme
Court together with *Miller*. All three argued that the Scottish Parliament,
the National Assembly for Wales and the Northern Ireland Assembly had to
consent to the invocation of Article 50.

In each case this was unanimously rejected by the court, confirming
the sovereignty of the Westminster Parliament over its devolved adminis-
trations, and the scope of legislative powers afforded to each.

## European Union (Withdrawal Agreement) Act 2020

The two years following the triggering of Article 50 by Theresa May
marked a very turbulent period in British politics. Suffice to say, it
resulted in May seeking extensions to the Article 50 withdrawal period,
as well as a General Election in June 2017 that returned her as prime
minister but with a reduced majority and a minority government. May
resigned as prime minister in June 2019, leading to the subsequent election of Boris Johnson as Conservative Party leader and prime minister
who called a General Election on December 2019 that returned his party
to government with an overwhelming majority to fulfil his manifesto
pledge to 'Get Brexit Done'.

Consequently, Johnson's government presented to Parliament the European Union (Withdrawal Agreement) Act 2020 on 19 December, seven
days after winning the General Election. This Act came from the Bill of
the same name in the previous Parliament that had reached its second-stage
reading but had been debated no further. Now including amendments from
the new Johnson government, the Act was passed through the Commons
and the Lords with little debate and became law on receiving Royal Assent
on 23 January 2020. Seven days later, at midnight on 31 January 2020,

the United Kingdom and Gibraltar officially withdrew from the European Union and entered a transition phase.

## Transition period

The reason for a transition phase until 31 December 2020 is to allow the United Kingdom and European Union to negotiate additional arrangements, primarily concerning trade. The current rules on trade, travel and business for the United Kingdom and European Union will apply during this transition period, with any new rules that are yet unknown taking effect on 1 January 2021.

And also why we must now turn back to look at the European Union proper as a source of Scots law.

## EC primary legislation: European Union Treaties

What we now call the European Union originally began life as the European Economic Community (EEC), established by the Treaty of Rome in 1957. The EEC itself was a logical extension, into other trade areas, of its forerunner the European Coal and Steel Community, which was established in 1951 between France, Belgium, the Netherlands, Italy, Luxembourg and West Germany. The main purpose of the emergent EEC was to bring about the harmonisation of its Member States' respective economic policies and the removal of international trade barriers between them. After initially regarding it with relative indifference, the United Kingdom finally became a member of the EEC in 1973.

The Treaty of Rome has been followed by other international agreements between Member States. The Single European Act 1986 established the European Community (EC) with the purpose of creating a single European internal market. This was followed by the Treaty on European Union 1992 (the 'Maastricht Treaty'), which led to the establishment of the European Union and with the view of facilitating increased social and political cohesion. Two further treaties – the Treaty of Amsterdam 1997 and the Treaty of Nice 2001 – were subsequently passed, primarily to address certain criticisms of the earlier Maastricht Treaty which was deemed too much of a political compromise. More recently, the Treaty of Lisbon which entered into force on 1 December 2009 helps provide the European Union with modern institutions and working methods more suited to the challenges of the world today.

The treaties referred to above can be considered the *primary legislation* of the European Union. This primary legislation has also given rise to a plethora of secondary legislation, which is crafted in different ways. It is worth noting that, despite the inception of the term 'European Union', such secondary legislation is generally referred to as 'European Community law' or 'EC legislation'. As one might imagine, and in common with UK and Scottish domestic secondary or delegated legislation, EC secondary legislation must not conflict with its treaties. In general, all EC law takes precedence over Member States' domestic law in each area. If there is any ambiguity between a point of EC law and its UK or Scottish equivalent, then EC provision takes precedence (*R* v *Secretary of State for Transport,* ex parte *Factortame* (1990)).

## EC secondary legislation

### Regulations

Regulations are binding on all Member States and are directly applicable to and on them without any need for enactment in the domestic law of the state concerned. This type of legislation must be published in the *Official Journal* of the European Union and will normally enter into effect on a date set out in the regulation itself.

### Direct effect

In EU law, *direct effect* is the principle that EU law may, if appropriately framed, confer rights on individuals that Member States' courts are bound to recognise and enforce in their favour. Direct effect is not explicitly stated in any of the EU treaties. Its principle was first established by the European Court of Justice (ECJ) in *Van Gend en Loos* v *Nederlandse Administratie der Belastingen* (1963). Direct effect has subsequently been loosened in its application to treaty articles. The ECJ has developed the principle holding that it can apply to other forms of EU legislation, such as its regulations and in certain circumstances its directives.

### Vertical direct effect and horizontal direct effect

In *Defrenne* v *SABENA* (No. 2), the ECJ decided that there were two varieties of direct effect: vertical direct effect; and horizontal direct effect. The distinction turning on the person or entity against whom the right enjoyed by the individual under EU law is to be enforced.

*Vertical direct effect* concerns the (vertical) relationship between EU law and a Member State's national law, specifically, the state's obligation to ensure its observance and its compatibility with EU law, thereby enabling citizens to rely on it in (vertical) actions against it, the state, or emanations of the state (i.e, its public bodies, as determined by *Foster* v *British Gas plc* (1990)).

*Horizontal direct effect* concerns the (horizontal) relationship between individuals, including companies. If a provision of EU law has horizontal direct effect, EU citizens can rely on it in actions against each other. While certain provisions of EC treaties and EU legislative acts such as regulations *are* capable of being directly enforced horizontally, it is worth noting that directives are usually incapable of horizontal direct effect.

### Regulations direct effect

Regulations are characterised by this important notion of 'direct effect'. Article 288 of the Treaty on the Functioning of the European Union states that a regulation 'shall be binding in its entirety and *directly* applicable in all Member States'. All regulations are thus directly effective and following *Antonio Muñoz y Cia SA and Superior Fruiticola* (2002) may *also* be *both* vertically and horizontally directly effective. This means that Scottish citizens can enforce *regulations* directly through the domestic courts of the land. In addition, given the supremacy of EC law, Member States are prohibited from enacting any domestic provisions contrary to the terms of the regulation.

An example is the European Union's regulation on Flight Delay Compensation that came into force on 17 February 2005. Under this particular regulation, minimum rights for passengers were ensured in all EU countries in cases where a flight is cancelled, delayed or a passenger is denied boarding. Passengers have recourse to national courts if these rights are not met.

The decision as to what form an EC law provision will take is normally left to the European Commission (see below).

### Directives

Directives, unlike regulations, do not automatically enter the domestic law of Member States. When a directive is passed, Member States are instead given a certain period within which to enact domestic legislation compatible with the aim of the directive. Consequently, a directive may be brought into force, domestically speaking, either by the passing of an Act of Parliament or by delegated legislation.

In the sphere of UK agency law, for example, the provisions of European Directive 86/653 were brought into force by the Commercial Agents (Council Directive) Regulations 1993 (a form of UK-delegated legislation). Similarly, the EU Working Time Directive 2003/88/EC enacted to update earlier versions from 2000 and 1993.

Directive 2003/88/EC gives EU workers the right to at least four weeks' paid holiday each year, rest breaks and rest of at least eleven hours in any twenty-four hours. It also restricts excessive night work, provides for a day off after a week's work and the right to work no more than forty-eight hours per week. Since excessive working time is cited as a major cause of stress, depression and illness, the purpose of the directive is to protect people's health and safety. Such, as is the norm with directives, was given effect in the United Kingdom with the Working Time Regulations Statutory Instrument 1998/1833. Readers should not confuse EC regulations with UK domestic regulations (statutory instruments made under delegated powers by ministers or public bodies – two of which are referred to above).

The UK domestic courts were encouraged by the House of Lords in its judicial capacity, and its successor the Supreme Court, to take a progressive approach in their interpretation of domestic legislation in that in seeking to implement a directive effect should be given by them to its *meaning*. In *Litster v Forth Dry Dock and Engineering Company Ltd* (1989), for example, the House of Lords was willing to write into domestic provisions words not approved by Parliament to give effect to the provisions of the directive concerned. In *Litster*, an hour before the sale by the receiver of the Forth Dry Dock and Engineering Company Ltd to the Forth Estuary Company, the receiver sacked all of its twelve employees. The new Forth Estuary Company had another set of employees already lined up on lower pay. The receivers had no money left to pay damages for dismissal and holiday pay.

Regulation 5(3) of the EU Transfer of Undertakings (Protection of Employment) Regulations (TUPER) 1981 states that its regulations on workers' rights in such circumstances apply to employees who are employees 'immediately before' the transfer (now, TUPER 2006, Regulation 4(3)).

The Court of Session held that none of the Forth Dry Dock and Engineering Company employees was employed 'immediately before' the transfer. The disgruntled employees then appealed to the Judicial Committee of the House of Lords. Here, Lord Templeman said in regard of Article 4 of the Business Transfers Directive 77/187/EC, that the 'courts of the United Kingdom are under a duty to follow the practice of the European Court of Justice by giving a purposive construction to Directives and to Regulations issued for the purpose of complying with [them]'. Consequently, the ECJ held that the Directive applied both to an employee at the transfer moment and to an employee who 'would have been so employed if he had not been unfairly dismissed in the circumstances described'. It was thus held that liability for unfair dismissal compensation transferred to the transferee – the Forth Estuary Company – and the employees of the Forth Dry Dock and Engineering Company were duly compensated.

## Directives and direct effect

In general, directives *do not* have direct effect. This means that parties are unable to enforce the provisions of a directive through the Scottish courts until the directive has been incorporated into domestic law. There have, however, been instances in which the ECJ has held that a citizen of a Member State could enforce a directive directly against a public body which was an organ, or *emanation*, of the state. This kind of right will arise in circumstances where the time limit for implementation of the directive has passed, but it has not yet been incorporated into the Member State's domestic law. For example, see Case 148/78 *Pubblico Ministero v Ratti* (1979); *Marshall v Southampton and South-West Hampshire Area Health Authority* (1986).

In the *Marshall* case, a female employee, who was being forced to retire at the age of 62 (when, at the time, the usual retirement age for men was 65), claimed that the health authority that employed her was acting in a discriminatory fashion contrary to (now) Article 141 of the EC Treaty and Equal Treatment Directive 76/207. The ECJ held that, as the authority was a public body, it was bound to act within the terms of the directive, even though its terms had not been enacted into domestic law.

The result of the above approach could be considered somewhat inequitable, given that it would allow, for example, an employee in the public sector to enforce a directive in such circumstances against his or her employer, but similar rights would not be available to an employee in the private sector. In view of this anomaly, the ECJ has also allowed directives to be directly enforced against private individuals and entities of Member States in circumstances having 'horizontal direct effect', although the case law to date can hardly be described as consistent (see, *von Colson and Kamann v Land Nordrhein-Westfalen* (1984); and compare with *Marleasing SA v La Comercial Internacional de Alimentacion SA* (C-106/89) (1992). See, further, *Unilever Italia SpA* (C-443/98) (2000)).

In addition, the ECJ has held that a citizen may bring an action for damages for the failure of his or her Member State to bring its domestic law into line with a directive (*Francovich v Italian Republic* (1992); *Dillenkofer v Federal Republic of Germany* (C-178-9/94) (1996); *Porter v Attorney-General for Northern Ireland* (settled out of court on 26 June 1995)).

## Decisions

Many hundreds of administrative decisions of the Commission or Council of Ministers are enacted annually. These decisions are addressed *either* to Member States *or* to specified corporations or individuals. Decisions do not require to be enacted into domestic law and have direct effect and are binding on the addressee alone.

An example of an EU decision, albeit a long-winded one, is the Commission Implementing Decision (EU) 2016/1189 of 19 July 2016 authorising the placing on the market of UV-treated milk as a novel food under Regulation (EC) No. 258/97.

## THE EC LAW-MAKING PROCESS

The EC law-making process is very unlike the United Kingdom's legislative procedures. EC legislation is crafted by a cumbersome interaction between three of the European Union's principal political organisations or 'institutions': the Commission; the Council of Ministers; and the European Parliament. The other two institutions are the ECJ and the Court of Auditors. The role of EU judicial bodies is discussed in Chapter 3.

### EU institutions

#### The European Commission

The European Commission comprises twenty-seven commissioners (one for each Member State), each responsible for a portfolio or area of EU activity (e.g., agriculture, climate action, competition, digitalisation and information, among others). Commissioners are EU nationals and act in an independent capacity from their Member States. This detachment of Commissioners from their respective homelands renders the Commission a pro-European body. The Commission has several functions, and primarily has responsibility for proposing new legislative measures. It can also be the guardian of its treaties and, for example, may raise an action against any Member State at the ECJ for their alleged failure to comply with treaty provisions.

#### The Council of Ministers

The Council of Ministers comprises ministerial representatives of the now twenty-seven Member States. Its composition may alter depending on the area of policy under discussion at its meetings. In practice, it is more concerned with safeguarding Member States' national interests than that of the overtly pro-EU European Commission. The Council is the supreme law-making body in the European Union and lies at the heart of the legislative procedures.

## The European Parliament

The European Parliament is the directly elected body of the European Union. In this sense, at least, it is a democratic body, although it is not the principal law-making body in the European Union in the same way that the UK Parliament is in respect of UK law. Prior to Brexit, some 751 members (known as Members of the European Parliament (MEPs)) were elected by the twenty-eight Member States on a constituency basis in national elections. With the United Kingdom's withdrawal from the European Union on 31 December 2019, this number has reduced to 678 MEPs from the remaining twenty-seven Member States.

Dependent on their size and, to an extent, political clout, Member States return between six and ninety-six MEPs. Until the United Kingdom left the European Union on 31 January 2020, it returned seventy-three MEPs. MEPs do not sit in national groups in the Parliament, but rather along political lines in 'blocs'. The Parliament, which is unicameral, or one-chamber in nature, is primarily an advisory body but, as discussed below, it does have a co-operative and consultative role to play in the legislative process which has, moreover, been strengthened in recent years.

## Law-making processes

Given the complexity of the law-making process within the European Union, the following discussion represents a mere snapshot. The Commission, as the Executive within the European Union, is responsible for proposing new legislative measures. In short, when a proposed measure is drafted by the Commission, it is sent to the Council of Ministers, and in turn forwarded to the Parliament. The Parliament may debate the measures and seek further representations from the Commission, and then provide advice as to the appropriateness of the proposals to the Council of Ministers. At this stage, the proposed legislation is scrutinised by a Council working group manned by civil servants drawn from all Member States. Ultimately, the decision to give the proposal binding force or not generally lies with the Council.

Despite the traditionally subservient role of the EU Parliament in the European community law-making process, its legislative powers were substantially enhanced under the Single European Act 1986. This treaty introduced a new co-operation procedure which allows the Parliament to either accept or take issue with the 'common position' taken by the Council. If the Parliament rejects the Council's position, this can only be ignored by the Council based on unanimity, meaning that all relevant ministers in the Council concur. In the case of any Parliament amendment to the common position, a qualified majority of the Council of Ministers may override their proposed amendment.

The Treaty on European Union 1992 gave the Parliament additional powers under the 'co-decision procedure'. This vested more substantial rights of consultation in the European Parliament and, in practice, may afford the Parliament a right of veto over a Council decision and, hence, block legislation. The European Parliament's legislative power was increased again in the aftermath of the Treaty of Nice 2001, which was brought into effect on 1 February 2003. One might expect that if closer political and social integration between Member States were ever to become a reality, the influence of the democratically elected Parliament would further increase.

## STATUTORY INTERPRETATION

The way in which statutes are interpreted has a major influence on the way in which legislation acts as a source of law. Statutory interpretation is therefore an important process by which, for example, a court must ascertain whether a piece of legislation applies to the facts at hand and, if so, what kind of effect that legislation has. If the issue is brought before a court, given that statutory interpretation is a question of law, it will always be determined by the judge and not the jury.

Many disputes that reach the civil courts in fact boil down to a disagreement over statutory interpretation. In an ideal world statute would be clear and precise, but even with the best of intentions (and the skill of parliamentary draftsmen and women) this is not always the case. Throughout the years, several rules have originated and been developed to assist courts in the interpretation of statutory terms that are thought to be confusing, nebulous or open to different interpretations. Given that words may hold different meanings, any form of verbal communication can be obscure at times – and legislation is no different. Most rules of statutory interpretation have been developed and refined by the courts themselves through the common law (for a discussion of common law sources, see below). A rare statutory intervention in this common law area is the Interpretation Act 1978. This Act provides scant assistance in most cases, however, and merely provides guidance of a general nature on the interpretation of words and phrases commonly used in legislation such as 'land', 'month' and 'sheriff'. The Act also allows certain assumptions to be drawn from wording in a piece of legislation unless the contrary is expressly stated in the statute concerned. So, for example, references in an Act to the masculine will be taken also to include the feminine; references to the singular will also include the plural; and references to persons will encompass both natural persons and artificial legal entities (e.g., corporations).

## Court rules of interpretation

From a constitutional perspective, the role of the courts is to apply the wishes of Parliament rather than deviate from statutes. As noted above, an Act may give rise to ambiguity, confusion and even, were the provision to be interpreted to the letter, absurdity. Against this backdrop, courts may at times take different approaches to interpreting statutes. Fundamentally, the two basic techniques that courts may choose when interpreting legislative provisions are known as the 'literal rule' and the 'liberal rule'.

### The literal rule

With the literal rule, the language in the Act is interpreted to the letter and not amplified in any sense by the court, even though this might lead to a somewhat illogical outcome that could not plausibly be said to have been the true intention of Parliament.

A stark example of an unsatisfactory literal interpretation can be seen in *Eddington* v *Robertson* (1895). At common law in the nineteenth century, a wife was entitled to a share of her husband's moveable estate if her husband died or divorced her. Moveable property is property that is not 'heritable', such as land and buildings. This general area of law was put onto a statutory footing by the Married Women's Property (Scotland) Act 1881, although, under the Act, such share in an estate was available only when the husband died. Even though the absence of a right to share in the estate on divorce in the statute had almost certainly been caused by a draftsman's error of omission, the court refused to amend the wording to grant a divorced wife a remedy previously allowed at common law.

Today it is likely the literal rule of statutory interpretation would be adopted only where the language in the statute under scrutiny was plain and unambiguous.

### The liberal rule

The liberal rule, in contrast, allows the court to look at the general policy underpinning the Act, in addition to the wording of the Act itself. This is to ascertain what Parliament intended and to hopefully provide a more satisfactory result, as exemplified by the court in *Bonsor* v *Musicians' Union* (1956). Bonsor had been expelled from the Musicians Union for falling behind in his membership subscriptions. It became difficult for him to get work as many venues only employed Musicians' Union members. He sued the Musicians' Union for damages, claiming his expulsion was *ultra vires*. It became important in the case to ascertain whether a trade union was a legal entity under the Trade Union Act 1871, and as a consequence of this interpretation what the was nature of the contract (if any existed) between Bonsor and the Musicians' Union.

To assist, the aims of Parliament are gauged, for example, by the examination of various external and internal aids (see below). Other techniques, such as the 'mischief rule' and the 'golden rule', may also be utilised in respect of statutory interpretation. However, these approaches are probably best viewed as mere variations of the two main literal or liberal rules.

## The mischief rule

The mischief rule prescribes that the court interpret the provisions of an Act by reference to both the Act's express terms and the '*mischief*', or the evil or problem that it was designed to alleviate (see *Corkery* v *Carpenter* (1950)). When applying the mischief rule, the court's role is to suppress the mischief at which the Act is aimed and advance the remedy.

An example can be found in *Smith v Hughes* (1960). The defendants were prostitutes who had been charged under the Street Offences Act 1959, which made it an offence to solicit in a public place. The prostitutes were soliciting from private premises in windows or on balconies, and so could be seen by the public. In applying the mischief rule, the court held that the activities of the defendants were within the 'mischief' at which the Street Offences Act was aimed, even though under a literal interpretation they would be in a private place.

## The golden rule

The golden rule holds that courts must give effect to the intention of Parliament by giving the terms of the Act their normal and common usage, except where such an approach would cause an obvious absurdity or inconsistency. In such a case, the court could then interpret the provision in a liberal manner.

A pertinent example of the application of the golden rule can be found in *Adler* v *George* (1964), where the court held literal statutory wording that read 'in the vicinity of' should be interpreted to include actions committed by the defendant within the area concerned, and not strictly speaking within its vicinity.

## Internal aids to interpretation

Help with interpretation may sometimes be derived from within the Act itself. For example, most recent Acts contain their own interpretation section which defines the terms that are thereafter used in the Act. Courts may also have recourse to the notion of 'interpretation in context', where a court may consider the statute to then interpret and better understand a particular part of it. Moreover, assistance may also be found in parts of the Act such as its title, long or short; any preamble to the Act; schedules to the Act; or any headings or subheadings therein.

## External aids to interpretation

The courts may also look to external aids to help assist their interpretation. These external sources include:

- any reports, such as those published by the Scottish Law Commission, that preceded the Act and were commissioned to discover the defects in the law that the Act in question sought to alleviate;

- reports of parliamentary debates in Hansard, which is the official record of debates and other proceedings in Parliament – although only in cases where the legislation in question is ambiguous, and the reference is to a statement made by a Minister which is sufficiently clear and precise to assist in the Court's interpretation (see *Pepper* v *Hart* (1993)); and

- other Acts on the same subject matter, the long-established and recognised use of the terms requiring interpretation, and views set out in esteemed textbooks.

## Presumptions

As a final aid to interpretation, and in the absence of any expressed intention to the contrary, general *presumptions* concerning the intention of Parliament can be made by the judge. These presumptions include that:

- UK legislation is not intended to contravene international law;

- the legislation does not intend to usurp the jurisdiction of the courts;

- legislation should not have a retrospective effect (although some statutes will expressly provide for such retroactivity, such as the War Damage Act 1965 and the War Crimes Act 1990);

- statutes that restrict liberty or impose taxes on the public are to be construed narrowly;

- it is presumed that the terms of statutes are not intended to be enforced against the Crown or its agents; and

- where the statute imposes criminal liability, unless the contrary is expressed, there is a presumption that *mens rea* (a guilty mind) is required for commission of the offence.

It is also worth noting that in accordance with s. 3 of the Human Rights Act 1998, all statutory provisions must be read in a way that is compatible with Convention rights.

## HUMAN RIGHTS AND SCOTS LAW

Following on from the above, particular mention must here be made of the impact of the European Convention on Human Rights (ECHR) and the Human Rights Act (HRA) 1998, and of the way that these legal provisions can be considered to be sources of Scots law. Although a mere Act of the UK Parliament, the effect of the HRA 1998 is to bestow itself with a special status as a source of law that provides a marked influence on Scots law in general. In short, the HRA 1998 partially incorporates the bulk of ECHR articles into domestic law, as illustrated below. Prior to further discussion of the HRA 1998 itself, however, it makes some sense to begin with a short précis of the ECHR.

### The European Convention on Human Rights

The ECHR is an international treaty, established in 1950 under the auspices of the Council of Europe. It sets out fundamental freedoms and basic human rights in the form of its treaty 'articles' and protocols, that were added at later dates after the inception of the treaty.

These fundamental, basic entitlements – which can be termed 'Convention rights' – are far-reaching and include:

- Article 2: the right to life;
- Article 3: prohibition of torture;
- Article 4: prohibition against slavery or forced labour;
- Article 5: right to liberty and security;
- Article 6: right to a fair trial;
- Article 7: no punishment without law;
- Article 8: right to respect for private and family life;
- Article 9: freedom of thought, conscience and religion;

- Article 10: freedom of expression;
- Article 11: freedom of assembly and association;
- Article 12: right to marry;
- Article 13: right to an effective remedy;
- Article 14: prohibition of discrimination;
- Article 1, Protocol 1: protection of property; and
- Article 2, Protocol 1: right to education.

In the aftermath of the Second World War, a Council of Europe was formed with the intention of establishing some form of minimum code of human rights for the people of Europe. Out of this collaborative effort was born the ECHR. The United Kingdom became a signatory to the ECHR in 1950, although the treaty did not come into force until 1953. It is important to note that, as the ECHR is an international treaty, it did not follow from its ratification that its terms would become part of UK domestic law. Thus, the ECHR is not in itself a formal source of Scots law (see *Kaur* v *Lord Advocate* (1980); *Moore* v *Secretary of State for Scotland* (1985)). However, the ECHR has a partial force in the sense that if there is any ambiguity as to particular UK legislation, Convention articles may be referred to as an aid to its statutory interpretation (*R* v *Secretary of State for the Home Department, ex parte Brind* (1991); *Anderson* v *HM Advocate* (1996)).

Under its international obligations, when the United Kingdom ratified the Convention it became bound to adhere to its terms, but the treaty's lack of status as a source of domestic law meant that individuals seeking to assert their Convention rights could not do so initially in the UK domestic courts. Individuals claiming a state abrogation of their human rights were therefore left with the unsavoury option of taking their case to the European Court of Human Rights in Strasbourg (and even this right of petition did not arise until 1966). Such a legal action could entail a long, arduous, expensive and often fruitless journey. So, in this sense, Convention rights in the United Kingdom could previously be considered somewhat illusory in nature and difficult to assert in practice.

## The Human Rights Act 1998

Subsequently, the legal landscape for those claiming that their human rights have been violated by the state was radically altered with the passing of the HRA 1998. The stated purpose of the HRA 1998 was to 'bring Convention Rights home'. This goal has since been achieved to a significant extent by the partial incorporation of the provisions of ECHR articles, and First and Sixth Protocols (with the exception of certain derogations and reservations) into UK domestic law through the HRA 1998.

The result today is that those seeking to rely on Convention rights may now do so through the domestic courts instead of having to go to Strasbourg. The principal way in which the Convention is incorporated into domestic law is set out in s. 6 of the HRA 1998, which stipulates that in general all public bodies must act in accordance with Convention rights. Public bodies include the Scottish Parliament, local authorities, government ministers and departments, but, as a sop to the notion of parliamentary supremacy, not the UK Parliament. The HRA 1998 also applies to bodies which, although, strictly speaking, not public in nature, nevertheless carry out public functions. The Convention rights can thus also apply to wholly private organisations that carry out public functions, but only in respect of such public functions and not their private activities.

An example of this kind of 'quasi-public' body, cited at the time the HRA 1998 was proceeding through the parliamentary process, was 'Railtrack' (at that time, in the private sector). In respect of its public functions as a railway regulator, Railtrack was bound under s. 6 to act in accordance with Convention rights; but in terms of its private commercial activities, it was not bound. In general, s. 6 means that an action can be brought by a disaffected member of the public against public (or quasi-public) bodies in respect of an alleged breach of Convention rights, even where this does not otherwise infringe the common law of the land. Moreover, given that courts and tribunals are themselves defined as public bodies, they are also bound under s. 6 to act in accordance with Convention rights; hence, these rights may also have an impact in relation to all matters determined by courts, including those where there are no public bodies or public functions involved. This is known as the 'horizontal effect' of the HRA 1998. There has been some doubt about how far this horizontal effect extends (for conflicting views, see, e.g., Sir William Wade (1998) and compare with Lord Justice R. Buxton (2000)). It seems that the horizontal effect of the HRA 1998 does not supply aggrieved parties with any new grounds of civil action, but the state of existing principles of common law must now be tempered by human rights considerations.

The HRA 1998 is designed in certain ways to take precedence over all other sources of law. For example, by virtue of s. 19, prior to the second reading of any UK parliamentary Bill, any government minister bringing the proposed legislation to the House *must* state that in his or her opinion the provisions of the Bill are not contrary to the terms of the ECHR. However, given parliamentary supremacy, UK Acts incompatible with the ECHR are *not* void – ministers may proceed with the proposed legislation even though its provisions are not wholly consistent with Convention rights. In this sense, court powers of review are limited merely to declaring that the Act is incompatible. The minister concerned may then rectify the anomaly by a special fast-track procedure, but he or she is not bound to do so.

So, in this way, despite the enactment of the HRA 1998, Convention rights are not quite synonymous with a written constitution, the terms of which could not be ignored by Parliament. Nevertheless, where the UK Parliament enacts (or fails to amend) legislation that is contrary to Convention rights, aggrieved individuals would still have the option of taking a case to court.

## The ECHR and Scotland

As one might expect, due to its devolved status, matters are different in respect of legislation of the Scottish Parliament. Under s. 31(1) of the Scotland Act 1998, the member of the Scottish government responsible for the introduction of any parliamentary Bill must affirm that its provisions do not breach Convention rights. Unlike its UK counterpart, however, the Scottish Parliament is *forbidden* to proceed with legislation which is contrary to Convention rights, and any Act passed may be subject to legal challenge in the Court of Session on that ground under the Scotland Act 1998, s. 57(2).

When the HRA 1998 was passed, it was felt to be highly controversial. A number of commentators voiced concerns that the Act would quickly come to be exploited by lawyers; either to take issue with the legitimate exercise of public functions or to find loopholes and spurious grounds of action under which their clients could slip through the legal net and avoid their criminal liability or civil responsibilities. Human rights issues have since significantly influenced public activities and judicial decision making. Human rights matters can now therefore be considered an integral part of legal reasoning; and it could be argued that those reservations concerning the advent of the HRA 1998 outlined above have not come to fruition (see, e.g., K. Starmer (2003)). However, the applicability of human rights-based remedies against public organs of the state in the domestic courts has proved a thorn in policymakers' sides. Witness, for example, the debacle surrounding the relationship between the appointment of temporary sheriffs and the Lord Advocate in Scotland. Such triggered a breach of Article 6 of the ECHR (the right to a fair trial) and led to the summary removal of these short-term, stopgap judges, who in fact had become key in propping up an over-burdened civil justice system (discussed further in Chapter 3).

Similarly, the Scottish Government found to both its own and the taxpayers' cost that the archaic practice of 'slopping out' in Scotland's prisons was contrary to the ECHR prohibition against inhumane treatment, which thus gave a right of financial compensation to prisoners. It is estimated that from 2004 £14.5 million has been awarded – an amount outwith the subsequent and necessary refurbishment of prison cells with toilets.

Another important court ruling in *Hirst* v *United Kingdom* (No. 2) (2005) heard in Strasbourg, held that the UK Home Secretary's policy of denying the right to vote to prisoners may be contrary to human rights. The court did not state that all prisoners should be given voting rights. Rather, it held that if the franchise was to be removed, then the measure needed to be compatible with Article 3 of the First Protocol. The Scottish Government initially concurred with the position of the Westminster Government not to grant voting rights to prisoners, with then Deputy Minister Nicola Sturgeon stated in debate in June 2013 during the Scottish Independence Referendum (Franchise) Bill (now an Act) that: 'The principle that a convicted prisoner loses certain rights for the duration of their custodial sentence is a fundamental and long-standing part of the prison process.' However, with the extension of more devolved powers to the Scottish Parliament on the passing of the Scotland Act 2016, and with the Scottish Parliament now able to decide who could vote in local and Scottish Parliamentary elections, the mood music at Holyrood changed.

The Scottish Parliament's Equalities and Human Rights Committee held an inquiry into prisoner voting in June 2017. In its report published in May 2018 it found that all prisoners should be allowed to vote in local and Scottish Parliament elections. Consequently, we now have the Scottish Elections (Franchise and Representation) Act 2020 giving short-term prisoners the vote in council and Holyrood elections. Its application was earlier piloted in the September 2019 Shetland by-election, where five eligible prisoners were able to exercise their franchise – by *postal* ballot!

## COMMON LAW

The term 'common law' in this context comes from the fact that this source of law was originally 'common' to the land. As far as Scotland is concerned, such laws evolved from old customary practices often influenced by, and sometimes imported from, external sources such as Roman law, Canon law and English law, which were accepted and upheld by the courts in particular cases. Indeed, many areas of Scots law (e.g., agency law, criminal law and arbitration) are not principally founded on statutory sources but largely stem from the common law.

## JUDICIAL PRECEDENT

The role of the courts is key in the development of the common law. Thus, the second major source of Scots law after legislation is the body of principles stemming from court decisions that we call 'judicial precedent'. Judicial precedents are rulings that courts have established, rather than law derived from parliamentary action and other legislative forms discussed above.

### Stare decisis

Common law develops and becomes a binding source of law because later courts generally follow previous court decisions. This is called 'stare decisis', the principle that future court decisions are bound by earlier decisions of superior courts. Where a prior judgment must be followed, the decision can be termed as 'binding' precedent. Influential decisions which do not require to be followed are known as 'persuasive precedent'.

### Precedent and inductive legal reasoning

Judicial precedent is a demonstration of inductive legal reasoning, where legal principles are induced from individual case decisions. As a result of its deductive heritage of Roman law, Scotland did not historically follow a strict system of judicial precedent akin to that which had developed in England. Indeed, many of the Scots institutional writers (see below) expressly rejected this approach. Principally caused by an increase in case reporting, and arguably the influence of the English-dominated House of Lords (sitting as a court), in the eighteenth century Scotland began gradually to adopt a more rigid system of judicial precedent. In 1828 the Court of Session accepted that a prior decision of it as a court was binding.

Court decisions are generally binding only when made by a superior court. Moreover, the present case must relate to the same point of law as dealt with by the previous court. Both these issues are now explored in more detail.

### The civil court hierarchy and precedent

The Scottish court structure is discussed in more detail in Chapter 3. Suffice, in terms of the civil court hierarchy as regards the United Kingdom, the ECJ sits at the top and its decisions (pertaining to interpretations of EC law) bind all courts in the United Kingdom, although the ECJ is itself not bound by its own previous decisions.

The Supreme Court (previously the House of Lords sitting as a court) will set precedents for Scotland only in relation to appeals deriving from the Scottish courts or those cases dealing with the interpretation of UK statutes that apply in Scotland. Again, similarly to the ECJ, the Supreme Court may choose not to follow its own previous decisions.

In Scotland, the Court of Session is divided into the Outer House (a court of first instance) and the Inner House (principally an appeal court). The decisions of the Inner House bind itself and the Outer House and the inferior Sheriff Courts below in the hierarchy. Where a decision has been reached by one Inner House division, however, it may be over-turned by a 'full bench' of seven Inner House judges. Principally because they represent the view of a single judge, Outer House and sheriff court judgments are never binding; but they may, however, be persuasive (the Court of Session is discussed in more detail in Chapter 3). While sheriff court decisions are never binding, since the establishment of the Sheriff Appeal Court in 2018, when sitting in a civil capacity it should be noted that its civil decisions set binding precedent in those courts inferior to it (fuller consideration of this is discussed in Chapter 3).

### The criminal court hierarchy and precedent

Judicial precedent is not so rigidly adhered to in the Scottish criminal courts. For example, the High Court of Justiciary, when sitting as an appeal court, can depart from its own previous decisions. Sheriff Courts are bound to follow decisions of the High Court sitting as an appeal court. Moreover, Sheriff Courts are likely to view decisions of single judges made at first instance in the High Court with respect and, in prac-tice, will generally adhere thereto, even though it would seem that they are not formally bound to do so.

### Cases to be 'in point'

Before a court is bound to adhere to a former decision, it must be dealing with the same point of law as in the previous case. This is termed as being 'in point' or 'on all fours'. When a case is in point it may be factually quite different to the previous case, but the fundamental issue is whether it concerns the same point of law on which the decision in the previous case turned upon or was decided. The point of law that was decided (e.g., a common law principle of contract law, or a particular interpretation of a provision in a statute) will decide how the current case ought to be resolved. This point of law can be termed the '*ratio decidendi*' or simply the '*ratio*'. It is only the *ratio* of a case that is binding.

## *Ratio decidendi* and *obiter dicta*

Determining the *ratio* of a case may be an art in itself. It may be hard to prise the *ratio* from all other aspects of the case debated by the court. It could be argued that some judges like to pontificate at length, and in any judgment the court may embark on a long and, at times, arduous journey into the various legal matters having some relevance to the case at hand. Many hypothetical matters, historical issues and ancillary legal points may be raised, debated and examined in fine detail by the judges.

All such other remarks and opinions made in the court's judgment, which fall outwith the true *ratio* of the case, may be termed '*obiter dicta*' or '*obiter*'. *Obiter* remarks are never binding as such, but they may be highly persuasive, particularly when made by a senior court.

## Decisions of foreign courts

In novel situations where Scots law sources are deficient, courts may have recourse to decisions taken by foreign courts. English decisions may be influential, especially in legal spheres such as commercial and industrial law where the law is broadly similar across the United Kingdom. As mentioned in Chapter 1, English law has been the cornerstone of a host of legal systems across the world, including many US states and Commonwealth countries; therefore, decisions of the courts and statutory rules in these jurisdictions may also be of relevance from time to time.

The Scottish courts may also examine other sources of the rules and principles of foreign legal systems – for example, legislation or legal writings, when Scots law does not provide a solution. Reference to legal writings on Roman law, historically influential on Scots law, may also be of import; albeit that the influence of Roman sources has dwindled in more modern times.

## Case reports

Clearly, if judicial precedent is to function, previous decisions and judgments must be recorded and be capable of being found to be used by both litigants and the courts. Beginning in Scotland with the development of 'practicks' – early notes on cases first made in the time of James V – different case-reporting series have become increasingly common in modern times.

In Scotland, a number of different series of case reports may be referred to by parties in the hope of finding precedents that will assist their legal case. The most authoritative series of Scottish case reports is the *Session Cases*, which report decisions (and judgments) of the Court of Session and Scottish appeals to the then House of Lords, and now the Supreme Court. Other reports include *Scottish Criminal Case Reports*, *Scottish Civil Law Reports*, *Greens Weekly Digest* and the *Scots Law Times*. In terms of finding cases, readers should note that court decisions are commonly (but not always) cited using the names of the parties, the year, the case reporting series and the page number at which the case can be found. So, for example, in *Woolfson* v *Strathclyde Regional Council* [1978] SC (HL) 90, the parties to the action were Woolfson and Strathclyde Regional Council; the year of the case was 1978; the case reporting series, *Session Cases* (denoted by 'SC') and the page number 90. 'HL' denotes its ultimate appeal to the then House of Lords sitting in a judicial capacity.

Many case reports are now accessible online via legal research packages such as Westlaw or LexisNexis. Students and practitioners alike can now avoid ploughing through dusty tomes in their law libraries and instead search across different case-reporting volumes at the strike of a key, which has made legal research a far less onerous process and has aided the development of the law through precedent in a number of areas.

## Precedent: advantages

The system of judicial precedent fulfils several important functions. Principally speaking, judicial precedent promotes certainty and fairness in the law. Without a system of precedent, the law would, in general, be more ambiguous and consequently it would be likely that more court actions would be brought because of conflicting views on the state of the law. Previously decided cases give disputing parties guidance on the respective strengths and weaknesses of their legal cases, which is often a reality check that limits litigation.

Judicial precedent is also fundamentally bound up with the principle of 'natural justice' – in particular, the notion that the law should be applied in the same way to all in society. Related to this is the idea that the lower courts are less likely to make errors in their interpretation of the law if they are handed down guidance established through precedents from the superior courts. It seems logical that more junior judges should benefit from the experience and skill of their senior colleagues. Linked to this is the idea that judicial precedent limits *arbitrariness*, that is the ability of the judge to deviate from recognised legal norms and impose his or her own subjective view as to what a legal principle should entail.

Judicial precedent also allows the law to develop incrementally in a uniform and logical manner, given that courts can apply and amplify recognised legal principles to meet novel scenarios. So, in this sense, the courts may fill gaps in the law until Parliament determines to intervene.

## Precedent: disadvantages

As a system, however, judicial precedent does have its drawbacks. Law may become too rigid and inflexible if courts become restrained by previous decisions, which may have been wrongly decided or are no longer relevant. As a pertinent example, laws which served to render a husband immune from any charge that he had raped his wife were arguably preserved by the system of judicial precedent at a time when social standards had shifted in such a way as to hold the rule wholly unacceptable.

Judicial precedent is not, in practice, always followed. For example, to avoid the impact of a previous, perhaps unpopular, decision, the court may strive to split hairs and find artificial distinctions with a previous decision that would normally be considered binding. More fundamentally, as alluded to above, it may not always be an easy task to ascertain the *ratio* of any case. In reaching a decision, judges may follow two or more legal principles in determining their decision, or in some cases, particularly found in old, sketchy judgments, perhaps no discernible legal rationale at all! In appeal cases, where there is more than one judge sitting, different judges may be in accord with each other but arrive at the same decision by different legal journeys, each deploying different *ratios*.

Finally, it should be noted that many judgments still in fact remain unreported and, thus, many precedents go unnoticed – this is unsatisfactory. The lack of a universal system of reporting leads to a haphazard system of legal development. Moreover, in practice, finding a precedent that might support a case may become no more than a random, chance activity.

## INSTITUTIONAL WRITERS

As noted in Chapter 1, beginning in the late seventeenth century and continuing through to the early nineteenth century, the works of eminent legal jurists or Scotland's 'institutional writers' were instrumental in charting the development of a maturing Scottish legal system. Their works provided comprehensive discussions of various tracts of Scots law and laid the foundations for modern Scots law in several areas. The works drew upon early decisions of the Scottish courts, Scottish customary practices, general principles of morality and reason and the laws of other jurisdictions including Roman law, Canon law and English law. The writings were so revered that they became for some time a formal source of Scots law.

However, with the exponential rise in legislation, coupled with the adoption of a strict system of judicial precedent and comprehensive case-reporting systems, the importance of institutional works as a formal source of law has diminished. Notwithstanding, if the law is otherwise found wanting, then a principle expounded by an institutional writer may still nowadays be considered as a valid source of law and may be cited in court as such. Institutional works are primarily of historical interest, especially in establishing the origins of many areas of Scots law, and in determining how the Scots legal system has been influenced by other schools of legal thinking.

The first institutional writing was Sir Thomas Craig's discussion of property law in the *Jus Feudale* of 1655. Scotland's most influential and important work, however, was penned by Viscount Stair (James Dalrymple). His *Institutions of Scots Law*, first published in 1681, is the cornerstone upon which much of Scots law was built. This monumental work spanned a wide array of areas of Scots law including that relating to the law of obligations, property and succession.

Other important institutional writers and writings include:

- Sir George Mackenzie, *The Laws and Customs of Scotland in Matters Criminal* (1678);
- Lord Bankton, *An Institute of the Laws of Scotland* (1751–3);
- Professor John Erskine, *An Institute of the Laws of Scotland* (1773);
- Baron David Hume, *Commentaries on the Law of Scotland respecting Crimes* (1797); and
- Professor George Bell, *Commentaries on the law of Scotland and on the Principles of Mercantile Jurisprudence* (1810), and *Principles of the Law of Scotland* (1829).

## MODERN WRITINGS

Textbooks, articles and other pieces of legal writing have become increasingly common over recent years. These kinds of non-institutional work cannot be said to represent formal legal sources of law; rather, they merely represent an author's opinion on aspects of the law. Despite this, in modern times, some of the more esteemed legal works are cited in court both by parties' legal representatives and by judges. Nevertheless, non-institutional works are only ever considered to be persuasive. Opinions of writers in influential texts may gain a legal authority, but such authority will merely stem from the fact that the court has approved that viewpoint. It is therefore the court's view that is the authority, and not, strictly speaking, the opinion of the writer.

## CUSTOM

As noted in Chapter 1, custom was, historically speaking, an important way in which Scots common law developed. It is possible that a custom can still be identified and viewed as a formal source of new law. Although in modern times this is something of a rarity, given that many customary practices have been assimilated into law either by court decisions or through legislation. Nevertheless, a custom may be recognised as a new source of law if it can be shown to have been acquiesced to for a substantial period of time; where it is well defined and certain; if it is fair and reasonable; and if it is not inconsistent with recognised principles of law.

One well-known case in which a party attempted to rely upon a custom as a valid source of law was *Bruce* v *Smith* (1890), where the owner of property adjacent to waters in which whaling took place claimed to hold a customary right to a share in the spoils of such activities. In this case, however, the test of reasonableness failed, and the custom was held not to represent the law.

In addition, customary practices may bestow legal rights to parties in individual cases. In business contracts, for example, commonly accepted customs and practices of trade may be implied into these agreements in the absence of any express reference thereto. For this to occur the customary rule must be widely accepted within the trade; be specific, reasonable and not overruled by any express terms of the contract. A case where a customary practice was held to be incorporated into a contract in this way is *Stirling Park and Co.* v *Digby Brown and Co.* (1995), where it was held that, by custom of trade, solicitors would become personally liable for certain fees owing to sheriff officers if their client failed to make the payment due to them.

Customary rights can also be seen within the sphere of land law: 'public rights of way' may arise, whereby members of the public may gain a customary right to walk across a piece of private land.

## EQUITY

While any modern society would hope that the notion of 'equity' or 'fairness' would be at the very heart of its laws, equity has a particular meaning as a source of law in itself. The Scottish legal system differs in this sense from the English system. In view of its somewhat rigid early legal antecedents, England historically developed a separate and distinct system of equity overseen by the Chancery Court to deal with equitable claims, where the law did not provide a remedy. Law and equity were never split in this manner in Scotland.

### Specific implement and interdict

For Scotland, equity in practice represents a mechanism by which harsher facets of the law can be softened. So, for example, Scottish courts developed equitable remedies to be granted to parties in deserving cases, including that of '*specific implement*', which is an order to carry out a particular act; and '*interdict*', being an order prohibiting a particular act.

In addition, the superior courts in Scotland (the Court of Session and the High Court of Justiciary) may have recourse to the *nobile officium* (literally, 'equitable power').

### Nobile officium

The *nobile officium* allows the court, albeit rarely, to grant a remedy, remove the entitlement to enforce a particular legal right, or deem a particular act a criminal one where it determines that it is equitable to do so; even where, strictly speaking, the law does not.

One of the best-known applications of the *nobile officium* occurred in *Khaliq* v *HM Advocate* (1984), where a shopkeeper was held guilty of selling kits designed for 'glue sniffing' to children. Although this conduct did not amount to an offence under the existing criminal law of Scotland, the High Court of Justiciary exercised its equitable power to render the Mr Khaliq's act criminal in the interests of public safety. While such judicial activism is rare, the *nobile officium* represents a (limited) law-making function within the courts.

## QUASI-SOURCES OF LAW

Codes of practice are examples of 'quasi-sources' of law. Being rules and principles, which are not themselves law but relate to the enforcement of law, may appear like law, and are sometimes treated as such. Such codes are generally brief, systematic and reasonably comprehensive sets of precepts produced by government or public regulators and are targeted to the public or a particular industry. They may be produced to encourage a particular activity to be carried out more safely or more effectively in some way, and tend to be written in a plain, understandable fashion rather than legal jargon. Codes of practice may be required or permitted by an Act of Parliament and sometimes require parliamentary approval. As a category of legislation, they are difficult to classify – such includes Government Circulars (often available from government websites); Rule Books (produced by the body concerned); and Codes (Codes of Practice under, for example, the Police and Criminal Evidence Act 1984 applicable in England, and the Highway Code, among others).

Codes have varying levels of enforceability. Some offer mere guidance and are not enforceable in any way – for example, the secretary of state's guidance in respect s. 125 of the Transport Act 1985, in relation to the establishment of a Disabled Persons Transport Advisory Committee. Others are indirectly enforceable in certain ways – for example, ss. 16 and 17 of the Health and Safety at Work etc. Act 1974 empowers the Health and Safety Executive, subject to the approval of the secretary of state, to create and issue Approved Codes of Practice (ACOPs) that it regards necessary to provide guidance on the application of the Act, and such regulations made under it. By virtue of s. 17, failure to observe the ACOP will not render that person liable to criminal or civil proceedings. However, if a criminal offence *is* alleged, any approved code may be cited in evidence, such as those concerning the Health and Safety at Work Act 1974. Furthermore, where there is a failure to comply with the code, an accused person may be required to illustrate that they adhered to the objectives of the code in a manner other than implementing the code. Similarly, in civil proceedings where negligence is alleged it appears that a failure to comply with the code may be used in evidence to support a civil case.

## Essential Facts

- Sources may denote historical, philosophical or formal sources of law.
- The term 'formal source' refers to the way in which a particular rule becomes binding.
- These formal sources can be divided into statutory sources and common law sources, including judicial precedent, institutional writings, custom and equity.
- The primary source of Scots law is legislation. There are a range of bodies now empowered to legislate for the people of Scotland, including the UK Parliament, the European Union, the Scottish Parliament, and many bodies and individuals delegated the right to legislate.
- The UK Parliament at Westminster is composed of two chambers: the elected House of Commons, or Lower House; and the non-elected House of Lords, the Upper House.
- Given that the United Kingdom is a parliamentary democracy, the UK Parliament is the supreme legislative body. However, since the late 1990s power has been voluntarily conceded (or devolved) to other bodies such as the Scottish Parliament in Edinburgh and the Welsh and Northern Ireland Assemblies in Cardiff and Belfast, respectively.
- The UK parliamentary process is complex and drawn out, involving both chambers of the House. Royal Assent of the monarch is required before an Act can become law. The bulk of legislation is promoted by the government in the House of Commons in terms of Public Bills that then go on to be Public Acts.
- The Scotland Act 1998 led to the inception of the Scottish Parliament, which is empowered to enact laws in 'devolved areas'. However, many more important policies issues are 'reserved to Westminster'.
- Delegated legislation may be subject to internal control within either the UK or Scottish Parliament and external control through the courts; although it has been argued that neither is generally effective in practice. The key test of delegated legislation is its legality.
- In modern times, EC legislation coming from the European Union has become a major source of Scots law. In general, it has dominance over domestic provisions of Scots law at present.

- While the primary sources of EC law are found in its treaties, secondary EC law is made by a complex interactive process between the European Commission, Council of Ministers and European Parliament.
- EC law may take several forms including regulations, directives and decisions. While regulations and decisions generally have direct effect, directives normally do not, and require to be brought into domestic law before they are enforceable in Scotland.
- While the United Kingdom officially left the European Union on 31 January 2019, its treaties, regulations, directives and decisions will continue to have effect in the United Kingdom during the Brexit transition period. Said, at the time of writing, to be on the 31 December, 2020
- Statutory interpretation is the process by which courts or a lawyer interpret statutory provisions and apply them to a given set of facts. Courts may take different approaches in their interpretation of statute applying the literal rule, the liberal rule, the golden rule and the mischief rule.
- The European Convention on Human Rights (ECHR) sets out fundamental rights and freedoms.
- The ECHR is not a formal source of Scots law but has been partially incorporated into domestic law by the Human Rights Act 1998. Scottish citizens can now generally enforce the terms of the Convention through the domestic courts against public bodies.
- Court decisions operate as a source of common law by way of judicial precedent which means that the decisions of superior courts become binding on inferior courts.
- A previous judgment will be binding only if the *ratio decidendi* (i.e., the legal principle upon which that case was decided) is the same as the *ratio* in the present case. All other matters referred to in the judgment are known as *obiter dicta* and are not binding.
- Historically, institutional writers produced works mapping out different areas of Scots law as it developed. Such works were traditionally important formal sources of law. They are of lesser importance now, given the modern impact of judicial precedent and legislation.
- A custom may be recognised as a source of new law where it is well established; recognised and practised; well defined and certain; fair and reasonable; and not contrary to established legal principles.

- Equity is a method by which the law can be softened in practice. Scottish courts have developed the equitable remedies of 'specific implement' and 'interdict'. Further, the superior Scottish courts have a limited power called the *nobile officium*. This allows them either to grant or deny a remedy; or hold that an act is a criminal one even if this does not, strictly speaking, represent the law.
- Quasi-sources of law include codes of practice which, although looking like law and often treated as such, often represent embellishments on, or explanations of, how laws can be applied in practice. They have varying levels of enforceability.

## Essential cases

*A* v *Scottish Ministers* (2001): example of a challenge to a Scottish Parliamentary Act after receiving Royal Assent; the Act was made retrospective and was challenged by judicial review on human rights grounds; action failed on basis that human rights complained about were not absolute and could be abrogated by the state in the interests of public safety.

*Litster* v *Forth Dry Dock and Engineering Company Ltd* (1989): in terms of EC law validity as a source of law, the House of Lords was willing to write into domestic provisions words not approved by Parliament in order to give effect to provisions of the directive concerned.

*Marshall* v *Southampton and South-West Hampshire Area Health Authority* (1986): a female employee, forced to retire aged sixty-two, claimed that her employer, the health authority, was acting in a discriminatory fashion contrary to Article 141 of EC Treaty and Equal Treatment Directive 76/207; the authority was a public body (and thus an *emanation* of the state who set it up), and was thus bound to act within terms of the directive, even though its terms had not been enacted into domestic law.

*Eddington* v *Robertson* (1895): a wife was entitled under common law to share of husband's moveable estate if he died or divorced her. Such common law was put on a statutory footing with the Married Women's Property (Scotland) Act 1881, that said a woman's share in the estate was available when the husband died. It did not mention 'on divorce'. This was felt to be an error of omission on the part of the Parliamentary draftsman. Notwithstanding, the court adopted the literal rule of statutory interpretation and refused to amend wording to grant the divorced wife a remedy.

*Adler* v *George* (1964): adopting the golden rule, and applying it to literal statutory wording that read 'in the vicinity of', the court here interpreted the wording to include actions committed within the 'area' concerned, and not, strictly speaking, within its vicinity. 'Vicinity' could be read as 'nearby'.

*Bruce* v *Smith* (1890): the owner of property adjacent to waters in which whaling took place sought to assert customary right to share in spoils of such activities; a test of reasonableness failed; custom did not represent the law.

*Khaliq* v *HM Advocate* (1984): a shopkeeper was found guilty of selling kits designed for 'glue sniffing' to children; although the conduct did not amount to offence under existing criminal law of Scotland, High Court of Justiciary exercised *nobile officium* to render the act criminal in the interests of public safety.

## Website resources

### Where does Scots law come from?

Shelter Scotland

https://scotland.shelter.org.uk/get_advice/advice_topics/ complaints_and_court_action/structure_of_the_scottish_legal_ system/where_does_scots_law_come_from

### How Scots law is made

Shelter Scotland

https://scotland.shelter.org.uk/get_advice/advice_topics/ complaints_and_court_action/structure_of_the_scottish_legal_ system/how_scots_law_is_made

### Understanding legislation

The National Archives

www.legislation.gov.uk/understanding-legislation

**Legislation: Scotland**
The National Archives
www.legislation.gov.uk/browse/scotland
**How does a Bill become law at Westminster?**
UK Parliament
www.parliament.uk/about/how/laws/passage-bill/
**Bills and legislation: Westminster**
UK Parliament
www.parliament.uk/business/bills-and-legislation/
**The legislative process: Holyrood**
The Scottish Parliament
www.parliament.scot/visitandlearn/18633.aspx
**Types of Bill: Holyrood**
The Scottish Parliament
www.parliament.scot/visitandlearn/Education/18640.aspx
**Stages of a Bill: Holyrood**
The Scottish Parliament
www.parliament.scot/visitandlearn/Education/18641.aspx
**Acts of the Scottish Parliament**
The National Archives
www.legislation.gov.uk/asp
**Delegated Legislation: Scotland**
The Scottish Parliament
www.parliament.scot/visitandlearn/60169.aspx
**EU Law**
The European Commission
https://ec.europa.eu/info/law_en
**A guide to statutory interpretation**
In Brief
www.inbrief.co.uk/legal-system/statutory-interpretation/
**Human Rights and Scots Law**
The Scottish Government
www.gov.scot/policies/human-rights/

**Precedent and Scots law**

Open Learn

www.open.edu/openlearn/ocw/mod/oucontent/view.
php?id=72115&section=1#

Copy and paste into your browser

**Institutional writers**

Open Learn

www.open.edu/openlearn/ocw/mod/oucontent/view.
php?id=72111&section=4.1

Copy and paste into your browser

**Custom as a source of law in Scotland**

Wiley Online Library

https://onlinelibrary.wiley.com/doi/pdf/10.1111/j.1468-2230.1964.
tb01029.x

Copy and paste into your browser

**What is the *nobile officium*?**

BBC News

www.bbc.co.uk/news/uk-scotland-49933273

---

Video resources

**What is the Scottish Parliament?**

https://youtu.be/3s60a01AFbY

**Role and powers of the Scottish Parliament**

https://youtu.be/tGWW1wrvus8

**How are MSPs elected to the Scottish Parliament?**

https://youtu.be/E--r8nj4aUY

**The role of the Westminster Parliament**

https://youtu.be/JsxHcXp8U0I

**Making law at Westminster**

https://youtu.be/Wuk3L3tknwg

**Different types of Parliamentary Bill**

https://youtu.be/LaFgWniqd2Y

**Introduction to delegated legislation**

https://youtu.be/rIWBbB2yBJA

**Types of delegated legislation: Orders in Council**

https://youtu.be/5cSv5IyLgBU

**Types of delegated legislation: statutory instruments**

https://youtu.be/qHNF_-RuF3Q

**Types of delegated legislation: byelaws**

https://youtu.be/0dnKBPy2xKQ

**Parliamentary control of delegated legislation**

https://youtu.be/wtT-FO5NXOI

**Judicial control of delegated legislation**

https://youtu.be/ijaUSpUh5vY

**EU institutions**

https://youtu.be/FTWahdj-GJA

**How does the EU pass new laws?**

https://youtu.be/8C0Kq7ioOpk

**What is the difference between EU directives, regulations and decisions?**

https://youtu.be/CZAC_uEJWfY

**Judicial precedent**

https://youtu.be/l457lq5rfNA

**Advantages and disadvantages of judicial precedent**

https://youtu.be/S2ztJBShamc

# 3   THE SCOTTISH JUDICIAL SYSTEM

This chapter provides a discussion of the Scottish judicial system including an overview of its workings, procedures, remedies, sanctions and enforcement mechanisms.

Before embarking on a detailed examination of different courts, it may first be useful to consider several fundamental issues about the Scottish judicial system in general.

## CIVIL AND CRIMINAL COURTS

In most modern systems of law there are, fundamentally, two types of court: the civil court; and the criminal court. Civil courts are provided by the state and act as a forum in which disputes over the civil law (i.e., non-criminal law issues) may be resolved. Civil courts are an avenue of last resort if parties find themselves unable to find a solution to their dispute by consensual means. Generally, in a civil court, one party is seeking to enforce a legal right in some way against another and will consequently be seeking a specified remedy from the civil court. In any litigation in the civil courts, the party raising the action is called the 'pursuer', and the party defending the action is called the 'defender'. While the civil courts commonly arbitrate disputes between two private individuals, at times the state may also be a party, acting neither as pursuer nor defender. In plain terms, after hearing both legal arguments and factual assertions from both parties, the court will rule in favour of one or other of the parties and either grant the remedy sought or deny that remedy.

Criminal courts are also provided by the state. Unlike civil courts, where proceedings are generally instigated by private parties, the criminal courts represent fora in which the state can raise legal proceedings against members of the public. Such an action is known as a 'prosecution' and may be raised against those alleged to have acted in a manner contrary to the criminal law of the land. As noted in Chapter 1, the criminal law sets down a minimum moral code or standard of behaviour required by the state. Any 'accused' person may be judged or 'tried' accordingly in the criminal courts. If an accused is found guilty of a crime, they may be punished, or 'sentenced', accordingly (sentencing is discussed in more detail later in this chapter).

## Scotland's *three* criminal court verdicts

There are three verdicts that can be passed against an accused person by a Scottish criminal court: guilty; not guilty; and not proven. The 'not proven' verdict – which leads to the acquittal of the accused – has long been a controversial one, criticised as ill-defined and unsatisfactory. In 2013 the then Scottish Parliament's Justice Secretary, SNP MSP Kenny MacAskill pushed for its abandonment under his Criminal Justice Scotland Bill, but it failed to come to fruition because of criticisms from the legal fraternity.

However, if one examines the criminal court process, it is perhaps the 'not guilty' verdict that is the illogical one. In criminal cases, the prosecution must attempt to prove the guilt of the offender beyond all reasonable doubt – there is no correlative duty imposed upon the defence to prove the innocence of the accused. In strict terms, the only question is whether guilt has been proven or not proven. If guilt is not established, it does not necessarily follow that the accused is not guilty, except perhaps in the sense that one is deemed innocent until proven guilty under the law.

## Adversarial court procedure

In both the civil and criminal courts, court procedure is 'adversarial'. What this means is that the parties must bring forth arguments of both fact and law. Each party, therefore, presents evidence of their, perhaps partisan, view of the facts of the case while also presenting legal arguments based on their interpretation of the particular rules of law central to the case that they seek to present (e.g., legislative sources or principles of common law). In general, unlike the situation in inquisitorial court systems found, for example, in continental Europe, there is no independent inquiry by the judge into the facts and law of the matter.

Determinations of the relevant law that applies to the case, such as statutory interpretation or application of established judicial precedent, are made by the presiding judge. Factual issues may in some cases also be determined by the judge, but in other cases – primarily in more serious criminal matters – the facts of the case are established by a jury of members of the public. These issues are discussed in more detail below.

## Standard of proof

One of the key differences between civil and criminal courts is the standard of proof required in each. For a finding of guilt to be held against an accused in a criminal action, the case must be proved against him or her 'beyond all reasonable doubt', whereas in a civil action the standard of proof that the court must find in order to rule in favour of one party over another is the lesser standard of 'on the balance of probabilities'.

## Corroboration

Similarly, there are different rules relating to the nature of evidence in both court arenas – the key one being that in a criminal case all essential facts must be corroborated or drawn from two or more independent sources, whereas there is no requirement for corroboration of evidence in civil matters.

Corroboration, like Scotland's 'not proven' verdict, has long been a subject of controversy. Again, in 2013, Justice Minister MacAskill called for its abolition, although plans for this were dropped by his successor Michael Matheson in 2015 as a consequence of subsequent criticism allowing for the Criminal Justice (Scotland) Bill introduced two years earlier to be passed into law as an Act of the Scottish Parliament.

## THE CIVIL COURTS

### Civil jurisdiction

As a primary rule, a court can only determine any action brought before it when it has the *jurisdiction* to do so. Jurisdiction must be held both in respect of the type of case brought before the court, and in relation to the parties to the action. In this latter sense, the court must hold jurisdiction over the defender under the doctrine *actor sequitur forum rei* (the pursuer is bound to 'follow the court of the defender'). Jurisdictional issues are discussed further below when examining the different civil courts.

There are three principal civil courts that hold jurisdiction in Scotland: the Sheriff Court; the Court of Session; and the Supreme Court of the United Kingdom.

### Sheriff Courts

Sheriff Courts are prevalent throughout Scotland. In terms of their organisational structure, sheriff court business is split into six geographical areas known as 'sheriffdoms'. Based upon Scotland's old, regional local government areas, the six sheriffdoms are: Grampian, Highland and Islands; Tayside, Central and Fife; Lothian and Borders; Glasgow and Strathkelvin; North Strathclyde; and South Strathclyde, Dumfries and Galloway.

As a result of the Shaping Scotland's Court Services Report by the Scottish Court Service presented in April 2015 to the Scottish Government, the six sheriffdoms saw a reduction in the number of sheriff court districts in Scotland from forty-nine to thirty-nine. Within each sheriff court district is a Sheriff Court and sheriffs. In total there are 142 permanent resident sheriffs who sit in Scotland's Sheriff Courts. Within each sheriffdom Sheriff Court business is organised and administered by a 'sheriff principal'.

Sheriffs principal and sheriffs are theoretically appointed by the monarch. In practice, however, the Queen acts on the recommendation of Scotland's First Minister, who acts on the recommendation of Scotland's Judicial Appointments Board. The First Minister is also bound to consult with the Lord President of the Court of Session under s. 95(4) of the Scotland Act 1998. Sheriffs must be solicitors or advocates of at least 10 years' standing (s. 5 of the Sheriff Courts (Scotland) Act 1971). Until the Courts Reform (Scotland) Act 2014 the sheriff principal had the power to appoint honorary sheriffs (Sheriff Courts (Scotland) Act 1907). Appointees were few and rare, but under s. 26 of the Courts Reform (Scotland) Act 2014 the position of honorary sheriff has since been abolished.

In the aftermath of the landmark court ruling in *Starrs v Ruxton* (2000), and further because of the Courts Reform (Scotland) Act 2014, the office of temporary sheriff was also abolished. The rationale behind this decision was essentially that the control over temporary sheriffs' appointment and reappointment exercised by the politically appointed Lord Advocate (as the head of the Scotland's Crown Office and Procurator Fiscal Service) was deemed contrary to the right to a fair trial enshrined in Article 6 of the European Convention on Human Rights (ECHR). It was argued that, as re-appointment was, in practice, at the whim of the Lord Advocate, this could lead to temporary sheriffs acting in such a way as to curry his or her favour.

Under the Courts Reform (Scotland) Act 2014, an additional twelve full-time and a large number of permanent part-time shrieval appointments were made in order to cover the immediate shortfall in judicial manpower that resulted from the abolition of temporary sheriffs, who, although initially employed as a stopgap, had over time become an integral cog in the Scottish civil justice machine.

Amongst the new appointments is a new category of judge, called a 'summary sheriff'. Summary sheriffs hear civil cases brought under 'simple procedure' and criminal cases brought under summary proceedings. Their sentencing powers are identical to a sheriff sitting in summary proceedings.

## Sheriff court jurisdiction

### Jurisdiction over the defender

Sheriff court jurisdiction over defenders can occur in different ways. In general, jurisdiction is governed under the Sheriff Courts (Scotland) Act 1907 and the Civil Jurisdiction and Judgments Act 1982 (as amended by the Civil Jurisdiction and Amendments Order 2001).

The court will hold jurisdiction over the defender where they:

- live in the sheriffdom (for at least forty days or have ceased to reside there for fewer than forty days and have no known address within Scotland – alternatively, if of no fixed abode, the defender may be 'personally cited' to appear in the court);
- carry on business in the sheriffdom (in which case they may be cited at their place of business);
- own, or are the tenant of, land or buildings within the sheriffdom, if the action relates to the property owned; or
- are involved in a contractual dispute where the contract was to be performed in the sheriffdom or the action relates to a delict (a civil legal wrong) which took place in the sheriffdom.

### Jurisdiction over subject matter

The Sheriff Court can hear all kinds of civil case, aside from a small category of claims that must be taken to the superior Court of Session, or cases in particular dispute areas that must be raised in tribunals and other specialist courts. In addition, the Sheriff Court holds exclusive (or 'privative') jurisdiction over particular cases.

## Lord Gill

At this juncture it is prescient to mention the recently retired former Lord President of the Court of Session and contemporaneous Lord Justice General Brian Gill.

In 2007, Lord Gill began a study into Scotland's civil justice system, culminating in the publication of his Scottish Civil Courts Review in 2009. It recommended substantial changes to modernise and improve the structure and operation of the civil courts, which he described as 'slow, inefficient and expensive'.

The report recommended that:

- cases of a value of £150,000 or more be dealt with by the Court of Session in Edinburgh;

- cases of a value of less than £150,000 be dealt with in the Sheriff Court;

- a new Sheriff Appeal Court be established to deal with appeals from the Sheriff Court and below, thus relieving the burden on the Court of Session as a court of appeal;

- the creation of district judges be introduced as a third-tier judiciary, dealing with civil claims valued under £5,000 and summary criminal cases;

- a specialist personal injury court be established in Edinburgh;

- a specialised procedure be established for multi-party class actions;

- active case management at all levels be implemented to improve process speed, court efficiency and expense; and

- a Civil Justice Council be established to monitor and develop the new system once in operation.

These proposals were welcomed by both the Scottish Government and the legal profession. Much of what Gill recommended came to fruition in the Courts Reform (Scotland) Act 2014, which was implemented in November 2016 after a transition phase. Of particular interest here are three of these proposals:

- the introduction of simple procedure in the Sheriff Court;

- the introduction of the Sheriff Appeal Court; and

- the All-Scotland Sheriff Personal Injury Court.

## Sheriff court procedures

Depending on the type of case being brought, the pursuer brings one of three types of claim to the Sheriff Court under its simple, summary cause or ordinary cause procedures.

### Simple procedure

At the bottom of the jurisdictional rung is the sheriff court simple procedure. Simple procedure came into effect in November 2016 following the Courts Reform (Scotland) Act 2014 and the Act of Sederunt (Simple Procedure) 2016 that operationalised it, as well as other new court procedures. Simple procedure replaced what was previously known as the 'small claims' procedure. The small claims procedure was itself introduced under the Law Reform (Miscellaneous Provisions) (Scotland) Act 1985.

Simple procedure is a similar court process designed to provide a speedy, inexpensive, and informal way to resolve disputes where the monetary value in dispute does not exceed £5,000. A claim is made in the Sheriff Court by a 'claimant'. The party against whom the claim is made is known as a 'respondent'. The final decision in a claim is made by a sheriff or a summary sheriff. This new simple procedure also, in large part, replaces summary cause, but only where it relates to actions for payment, delivery or for recovery of possession of moveable property, or actions that order someone to do something specific. In such instances, simple procedure is appropriate only where there is an alternative claim for payment for a sum of £5,000 or less, otherwise summary cause procedure should be followed.

The simple procedure is the most truncated and, at least in theory, informal of the procedures found in Scotland's Sheriff Courts. For example, some of the strict legal rules pertaining to the admissibility of evidence which apply to other court proceedings are relaxed. The idea of simple procedure is that the informality of the proceedings will mean that the process will be both speedy and more cost-effective, with the parties not requiring lawyers and hence saving on legal costs. Generally, no state-provided financial assistance or 'legal aid' to help a party engage a lawyer is available in simple procedure. Previously, it has been argued that its predecessor – the small claims procedure – was not always run in an informal fashion and may in practice have mirrored judicial proceedings in other civil courts (see Mays and Clark, 'ADR and the Courts' (1997) 2 SLPQ 57). Whether simple procedure will do likewise may be something to revisit in the future.

The cost of raising a court action using simple procedure depends on the value claimed. At the time of writing the fees are:

- £19 – for claims of £300 or less; and
- £104 – for claims over £300.

If a sheriff officer is used to serve the claim form on a respondent, this will cost £13 plus the sheriff officer's fees. To appeal a court decision there is a £61 fee.

Under simple procedure, legal expense claims and associated costs are possible against the other party. Scotland (as well as England) generally operates a 'loser pays' rule in civil legal proceedings. The same applies in simple procedure; however, such claims are capped according to a formula. If the value of a simple procedure claim is £3,000 or less, then awards of expenses to the 'winning' party made by the court are subject to the following statutory caps:

- no expenses are recoverable – for claims of £200 or less;
- a maximum of £150 – for claims of £200 to £1,500;
- a maximum award of 10 per cent of the sum claimed – for claims of £1,501 to £3,000; and
- no cap on award of expenses – for claims of £3,001 to £5,000.

## Summary cause

The summary cause procedure is governed by the Sheriff Courts (Scotland) Act 1971 (however, the latest rules were put in place in 2002 by way of the Act of Sederunt (Summary Cause Rules) 2002 No. 132). A summary cause must be raised where the monetary value sought is between £3,000 and £5,000 and for actions pertaining to recovery of possession of heritable property. From 2015, as just one consequence of the Gill Reforms, personal injury claims for damages are heard at the All-Scotland Sheriff Personal Injury Court in Edinburgh.

Reflecting the limited importance of the types of action brought thereunder, the summary cause, as its name suggests, is a shortened form of court process, where some of the general strict court procedural rules are relaxed. Actions may be raised by the *pursuer* completing a pre-printed claim form. If the *defender* does not return the form by a particular date (known as the 'return day') the court will automatically grant a decree in favour of the pursuer (although actions relating to eviction from heritable property do not have return days). Where the claim is timeously defended then a trial date (known as a 'proof') is set for a subsequent date to consider the case in full.

## Ordinary cause

Any other civil court action brought in the Sheriff Court where the value of the claim is over £5,000 is raised as an 'ordinary cause'. It is also the procedure used in the Sheriff Court for other actions – examples include family actions such as divorce, dissolution of civil partnerships and applications for orders relating to children (e.g., residence and contact).

The court procedure inherent in ordinary cause is provided for by the Sheriff Courts (Scotland) Act 1907 and represents the most formal, complex and, hence (in practice), most costly process in the Sheriff Court. An ordinary cause is brought by the lodging of a document known as an 'initial writ', which maps out the pursuer's grounds of claim in both legal and factual assertions. Where an action is to be defended, the initial writ is met by a set of answers known as 'defences' lodged by the defender. What follows is a negotiation period during which 'adjustments' to the legal and factual issues in dispute can be made by the parties. These might include admissions from either side and agreements on certain matters arrived at between the disputing parties. Any remaining grounds of dispute are determined at an 'options' hearing where the future procedure for resolving the dispute is set out. If necessary, the matter may then proceed to trial (or 'proof') before the court.

## Sheriff Appeal Court

Parties dissatisfied with decisions made by sheriffs may have a right to appeal. Gill's influence here has also become apparent with the recent creation of the Sheriff Appeal Court. First established in 2015 to hear criminal appeals, on 1 September 2018 the Sheriff Appeal Court's jurisdiction was extended to hear civil appeals. Before that date civil appeals were heard either by the sheriff principal for each sheriffdom or by the Inner House of the Court of Session.

A bench of three Appeal Sheriffs sit to hear appeals on civil cases raised under ordinary cause, with summary cause, small claims and procedural business decided by a single Appeal Sheriff. Appeals from the Sheriff Appeal Court are heard at the Court of Session. However, cases from here can only be appealed to the Inner House with the permission of either the Sheriff Appeal Court or the Court of Session itself.

With an eye to earlier discussion on precedent in Chapter 2, it should be noted that all judgments of the Sheriff Appeal Court in civil cases establish thereafter *binding precedent* on all sheriffs and in all sheriffdoms throughout Scotland.

## Court of Session

The Court of Session sits permanently in Edinburgh. It is divided into two houses: the 'Outer House', a court of the first instance in which cases may be raised for the first time; and the 'Inner House', primarily an appeal court.

As noted in Chapter 1, the Court of Session, as Scotland's first permanent court, is an institution with a significant history. Established in 1532, the court has seen radical reform over the years; although its present composition was created largely in the early nineteenth century, and its current procedures are principally regulated by the Court of Session Act 1988.

## Court of Session jurisdiction

### Jurisdiction over the defender

Jurisdictional issues are governed by the Civil Jurisdiction and Judgments Act 1982. Unlike the situation regarding the Sheriff Courts, the Court of Session holds jurisdiction over the whole of Scotland. The court follows the general rule regarding jurisdiction, in that the key issue in determining it is whether the court holds some authority over the defender. The principal method by which jurisdiction is found over a defender is that he or she is permanently or habitually resident in Scotland. If this is not possible, jurisdiction may be claimed on the basis that the defender is the tenant or owner of heritable property in Scotland, although it is not necessary for the action to relate to that property.

Jurisdictional rules arise in respect of consistorial matters, being matrimonial actions such as divorce, legal separation and nullity of marriage. In such instances, the court may exert jurisdiction when either party to the marriage in question has a permanent home in Scotland on the date that the action commenced, or was habitually resident in Scotland for one year immediately prior to the commencement of proceedings.

### Jurisdiction over the subject-matter

Certain cases (e.g., those where the monetary value of the claim is £5,000 or less) must be raised in the appropriate Sheriff Court. The Sheriff Court was given a concurrent jurisdiction to hear divorce cases in 1984, but it should be noted that a small category of cases remain that must be raised in the Court of Session, including those relating to personal status, actions of reduction, actions relating to the tenor of lost documents and judicial review petitions. Moreover, in civil matters where a party seeks recourse to the court's *nobile officium* (or 'equitable power'), this remedy is available only in the Court of Session.

There is significant overlap regarding the jurisdiction of the Sheriff Court and of the Court of Session. In the majority of civil cases, a pursuer is at liberty to choose between raising an action in the Court of Session and raising it in the local Sheriff Court. In cases which are of greater importance legally or financially, the Court of Session may be the more attractive option as this court has a higher legal status, which may mean that its decisions are less likely to be appealed. On the downside, however, given the generally more protracted nature of Court of Session procedures, and despite procedural matters having been improved of late, litigation at the Court of Session is likely to incur more time and greater costs than an equivalent action in the Sheriff Court. In addition, parties will be required to attend the court in

Edinburgh at stages of the litigation process, which may be less convenient than attending their local Sheriff Court. Moreover, litigants will be required to engage advocates or solicitor-advocates in addition to solicitors to represent them in the Court of Session, substantially increasing the financial burden of the action.

## Court of Session

### Outer House

Cases in the Outer House are heard by a single judge, known as a 'Lord Ordinary', who generally sits alone with no jury. Juries in civil trials have been largely abolished and are now entirely absent from civil sheriff court proceedings; however, a remnant of the past may be found in industrial accidents claims in the Outer House, where a jury of twelve may sit to deliberate over the facts of the case. Although recruitment to the judiciary is examined elsewhere in this book, it is worth noting here that Lords Ordinary are former legal practitioners, either suitably experienced Queen's Counsel (QCs), former sheriffs of five years' standing or solicitor-advocates of five years' standing. Recently, the number of judges has increased to help shore up the somewhat creaking Scottish civil justice system. At the time of writing, there are twenty-four Outer House judges in the Court of Session.

### Outer House procedure

Civil actions in the Outer House are normally commenced by one party lodging a written *summons* mapping out the principal legal and factual grounds of claim. If the other party to the case seeks to defend the action, this is done by lodging a corresponding set of *defences*. In a similar process to that found in the sheriff court ordinary cause, the parties then enter a period where they adjust the pleadings between them, during which grounds of dispute may be refined and narrowed. This is known as the 'open record'. When adjustments come to an end the *record* is said to be *closed*. The case may then proceed to a *proof*, being a trial to determine the facts of the case; or else a hearing may be required to be held to first determine certain legal issues which must be resolved prior to proof. In addition, there may be other occasions where it is necessary for the court to ascertain particular facts of the case before it can proceed to legal argument. This kind of hearing is known as a 'proof before answer'.

Further, certain actions are brought by *petition*. Basic examples include actions for the court to appoint new trustees or wind up a company or partnership. These are usually brought by one party – the *petitioner* – petitioning the court for a remedy to the situation that only the court can grant. The court may, where appropriate, remit the petition to a suitably qualified third party to determine the merits of the case sought, who then reports back to the court. In particular instances, such as an action by, for example, minority shareholders in a company seeking a remedy against majority shareholders, the petition may be contentious and, in this type of case, on receipt of the petition, the court may determine which of the majority shareholding parties should receive notice of it. Such parties, known as the 'respondents', may then have the option of defending the petition in court.

### Appeals from the Outer House

Decisions of the Outer House may be appealed to the Inner House by what is called a 'reclaiming motion'. Appeals are normally made on a point of law, although, rarely, an appeal may be heard on the facts. The appeal procedure is discussed further below.

### The Inner House

The Inner House is an appeal court, although it has a small *first-instance* jurisdiction to provide litigants with interpretations on points of law (e.g., in taxation cases and certain petitions by limited companies). The Inner House hears appeals from the Outer House, Sheriff Courts and other tribunals. There are two divisions in the Inner House: the First Division, comprising the Lord President (Scotland's senior judge) and four other judges known as 'Lords of Session'; and the Second Division, made up of the Lord Justice-Clerk (depute to the Lord President) and five Lords of Session.

In hearing any appeal, normally either division may sit with three judges present without any jury. In matters of particular import, the court may sit as a 'full bench' of seven judges. This number may also be expanded by including further judges from the Outer House. In busier times an Extra Division of Outer House judges may be convened to help expedite business through the Inner House.

### Inner House procedure

Appeals on the facts of cases are rare. The court is usually concerned with hearing arguments over disputed points of law (e.g., an interpretation of a statutory provision or common law doctrine) which determined how the decision of the previous court was arrived at.

After hearing an appeal, judges may deliver an instant decision orally or, more commonly, may adjourn the hearing (known as 'making *avizandum*') and issue a written opinion at some later date. In practice it is common for one of the judges to deliver an extensive, detailed written opinion. Commonly, the other judges will simply issue supplementary, 'concurring' judgments, which may merely stipulate that the judge has had the opportunity to read his or her colleague's opinion and agrees with it. With decisions taken by majority, judges are, however, sometimes in disagreement. In such a case, a judge may issue a 'dissenting' opinion. The decision of the court may be either to dismiss the appeal by 'adhering' to the decision of the previous trial judge or, alternatively, to uphold the appeal by 'recalling' the decision of the trial judge and substituting a new one.

## Appeals from the Inner House

Parties unhappy with the decision or 'interlocutor' issued by the Inner House may have a further right of appeal to the UK Supreme Court. This procedure – which is generally available only on a point of law – follows upon a petition 'praying' that the Supreme Court reverse the previous decision. Generally, this right arises only when the Court of Session grants leave to appeal. Leave is not required where the Inner House decision is not unanimous.

## Judicial Committee of the House of Lords

Until its abolition under the Constitutional Reform Act 2005 and its replacement in 2009 by the UK Supreme Court, the Judicial Committee of the House of Lords had the capacity to hear appeals from Scottish civil courts. It comprised the Lord Chancellor and several 'Lords of Appeal in Ordinary'. These eminent law lords based at Westminster had either held high judicial office or previously been barristers or advocates of at least fifteen years' standing (however, in practice, generally for a much longer period).

Despite controversy regarding the legal basis of this practice, the right of appeal to the Lords was first established in *Greenshields* v *Magistrates of Edinburgh* (1710–11). A significant criticism of the system, however, was that although the judicial committee by convention must have included lawyers of a Scottish ilk, there was no rule that any Scottish law lord should sit on a civil appeal from the Scottish courts. As noted in Chapter 1, concerns were raised over the years that led, on occasion, to the erroneous imposition of English legal principles on Scots law, and some say contributed to its demise. The extent to which this is true is, perhaps, debateable (for a detailed discussion see Paterson, Bates and Poustie (1999, pp. 91–4)).

Any decision by the House of Lords was given legal force only when the judgment was applied in the Inner House of the Court of Session. Although the quorum of judges was three, in practice it was usual for a panel of five judges to hear the appeal. In an effort to provide a more representative higher-tier judiciary, and separate the function of the judiciary from the influence of the executive, Part 3, Section 23(1) of the above Constitutional Reform Act created the Supreme Court of the United Kingdom in 2009, which replaced the House of Lords as a final court of appeal. The Supreme Court also assimilated many of the functions of the Privy Council. The Act also put an end to the previous judicial role of the Lord Chancellor and the Law Lords.

## THE SUPREME COURT OF THE UNITED KINGDOM

The Supreme Court is now the final and ultimate court of appeal in the United Kingdom for civil cases. It also hears appeals in criminal cases from England, Wales and Northern Ireland, and cases of public or constitutional importance affecting the whole United Kingdom.

Cases involving 'devolution issues' arising from the Scotland Act 1998 concerning the validity of Acts of the Scottish Parliament, or questions arising over executive functions of the Scottish Government are heard by the Supreme Court. Such cases may reach the Court after referral by the Advocate General. The Advocate General is one of the Law Officers of the Crown, whose duty it is to advise the Crown and UK Government at Westminster on Scots Law. An excellent if complex example of this is the UK Withdrawal from the European Union (Legal Continuity) (Scotland) Bill in A Reference made by the Attorney General and the Advocate General for Scotland to the Supreme Court in 2018. The question they asked was whether the Scottish Parliament has power to legislate for the continuity of laws relating to devolved matters in Scotland that are presently the subject of EU law but which will cease to have effect after the United Kingdom eventually withdraws from the European Union following the EU Referendum on 23 June 2016.

In a seven Bench decision, the Supreme Court held that parts of the Scottish Parliament's UK Withdrawal from the European Union (Legal Continuity) (Scotland) Bill were outwith its legal competence. S. 17 of the Bill erroneously amended the Scotland Act of 1998, impliedly giving the Scottish Parliament more powers than it was granted originally – such, they unanimously determined, was *ultra vires*.

Because of Part 4 of the Scotland Act 2012, the Supreme Court also has jurisdiction to decide on 'compatibility issues' that may arise as a consequence of s. 288ZA(2) of the Criminal Procedure (Scotland) Act 1995. These concern the compatibility of any aspect of a criminal trial in Scotland with the ECHR or EU law.

The impact of Supreme Court decisions thus extends far beyond the parties involved in any given case, shaping our society and directly affecting our everyday lives.

## Independence and transparency

The Supreme Court came into being in 2005 to achieve separation between the United Kingdom's senior judges and the Upper House of Parliament. The reason being was to emphasise the independence of the Law Lords from the political process and increase transparency between Parliament and the courts. In August 2009, the new Supreme Court Justices moved out of the House of Lords into their own building on the opposite side of Parliament Square. They sat for the first time as a Supreme Court in October 2009. In their first legal year, the Supreme Court gave landmark rulings on access to legal advice for Scottish suspects, the rights of gay asylum seekers, and the weight to be given to pre-nuptial agreements.

The Supreme Court, as well as being the final court of appeal, plays an important role in the development of UK law. As an appeal court, the Supreme Court cannot consider a case unless a relevant order has been made in a lower court (found listed online at: www.supremecourt.uk/docs/a-guide-to-bringing-a-case-to-the-supreme-court.pdf).

## Appeals from the Court of Session in Scotland

An appeal is possible to the Supreme Court from any order or judgment of a court in Scotland. As a rule, permission to appeal is not required from an interlocutor, or decree by a judge of the Inner House of the Court of Session on the *whole* merits of the cause. Such an appeal must be filed within forty-two days of the date on which the interlocutor appealed. Notice of appeal must be signed by two Scottish counsel who must also certify that the appeal is reasonable. Similarly, permission to appeal is not required from an interlocutory judgment of the Court of Session where there is a difference of opinion among the judges, or where the interlocutory judgment is one sustaining a dilatory defence dismissing the action. Again, the appeal must be filed within forty-two days of the date on which the interlocutor appealed; and the notice of appeal must be signed by two Scottish counsel who must also certify that the appeal is reasonable.

Permission to appeal *is* required for an appeal to the Supreme Court against any interlocutory judgment of the Court of Session that does not fall within the parameters laid out above. Here, only the Inner House of the Court of Session may grant permission to appeal. A refusal by the Court of Session to grant permission to appeal is final and no appeal may then be made to the Supreme Court. Permission to appeal from the Court of Session is also required for an appeal to the Supreme Court under the provisions of certain Acts of Parliament, and permission may be granted either by the Court of Session or, if refused by the Court of Session, by the Supreme Court. When permission to appeal under these circumstances is granted it is not necessary for two Scottish counsel to certify that the appeal is reasonable.

## COURT OF JUSTICE OF THE EUROPEAN UNION

As noted in Chapter 2, the purpose of the Court of Justice of the European Union (CJEU) is to ensure the compliance of EU Member States with the European treaties and secondary legislation enacted by the European Union. The CJEU is the chief judicial authority of the European Union and oversees the uniform application and interpretation of EU law in co-operation with the national judiciary of its Member States. The CJEU also resolves legal disputes between national governments and EU institutions and may act against EU institutions on behalf of individuals, companies or organisations whose rights have been infringed.

The CJEU is based in Luxembourg and is split into two Courts:

- **the Court of Justice (ECJ)** – which deals with requests for preliminary rulings from national courts, certain actions for annulment and appeals; and

- **the General Court** – which rules on actions for annulment brought by individuals, companies and, in some cases, EU governments. In practice, this means that this court deals mainly with competition law, state aid, trade, agriculture and trademarks.

### Court of Justice

The Court of Justice of the CJEU was established in 1952. Often abbreviated as the 'ECJ', it is composed of one judge per member state. The judges are assisted by eleven advocates general. The advocates general – who have no counterpart in the domestic courts of Scotland – are a demonstration of the inquisitorial nature of ECJ procedures. Advocates general are court officials who provide advice to the judges in the form of a detailed opinion on the legal issues at hand. Both judges and advocates general are appointed for a six-year period. The court very occasionally sits 'in plenary', which means that all twenty-seven judges of the court hear the case, but it is much more typical for cases to be decided in chambers in front of three, five or seven judges. The court also encompasses a Grand Chamber, comprising eleven judges that can sit whenever requested by a Member State or EC institution that is a party to proceedings.

The domestic Scottish courts can, at the time of writing, refer a point of EC law that is central to the deliberations in a current case to the ECJ.

Moreover, any court or tribunal from which there is no right of appeal in Scotland is bound to refer any interpretation of a point of EC law to the ECJ. Any ECJ judgments become legally enforceable only by their implementation in the domestic courts of the Member State concerned. In addition to dealing with referrals from the domestic courts of Member States, the ECJ has jurisdiction in a number of other EC matters, including taking action against Member States which are in violation of EC law; and in judicial review of possibly inviolate acts of EU institutions.

## General Court

The General Court (sometimes abbreviated as 'EGC') is also a constituent court of the CJEU. It hears actions taken against the institutions of the European Union by individuals and Member States, although certain matters are reserved for the ECJ. As a court of first instance, General Court decisions can be appealed to the ECJ, but only on a point of law.

Prior to the Lisbon Treaty of 1 December 2009, the General Court was known as the 'Court of First Instance'. The Court of First Instance had been established in 1988 because of the Single European Act. There are no permanent advocates general attached to the General Court (unlike the ECJ, which has eleven). However, the task of an advocate general may very occasionally be performed in a limited number of cases by a judge nominated to do so.

## CIVIL COURT REMEDIES

There are several remedies that civil courts in Scotland may grant, including the following:

- **Specific implement** – a specific implement is an order to carry out a particular act (e.g., performance of an obligation under a contract).
- **Interdict** – an interdict is an order prohibiting the commission or continuation of an act (e.g., the publication of a defamatory

article). An 'interim interdict' is a temporary interdict or stopping order pending a full court hearing dealing with the matter complained about.

- **Damages** – damages is an order that sees one party pay financial compensation to the other commensurate with any loss or injury sustained.

- **Declarator** – a declarator is a declaration that a party has a specific right or duty.

- **Reduction** – a reduction is an order that the terms of an invalid document (e.g., a will) are set aside.

- **Aliment** – an aliment is an order to provide financial support to a spouse (e.g., in a divorce action).

There are also several other remedies at Scotland's civil court's disposal that might apply in, for example, the legal separation or divorce of married couples.

## DILIGENCE AND THE CIVIL COURTS

To aid in the enforcement of court orders and decrees for financial compensation and payments of debts due to creditors, different types of 'diligence' may be employed by the civil courts that see the 'freezing' of the debtor's property and often, ultimately, the sale of the same to make good the debt due. Below represents an overview of the main diligence procedures that creditors may have recourse to use. As many creditors do, in that Scotland's insolvency agency Accountant in Bankruptcy reported 260,835 diligences executed through Scotland's Sheriff Courts in 2018–19; a 4.1 per cent increase on the previous year.

### Accountant in Bankruptcy

Accountant in Bankruptcy is an executive agency of the Scottish Government responsible for administering the process of personal bankruptcy and recording corporate insolvencies in Scotland. It is responsible for the determination of personal and entity bankruptcy applications, making decisions on debt payment programme applications under the Debt Arrangement Scheme and protecting trust deeds.

All bankruptcies, trust deeds and statutory debt payment programmes are recorded in public registers maintained by the agency along with details of corporate liquidations and receiverships.

## Diligence procedures

A creditor can exercise diligence if a debtor has fallen behind with payments towards a debt by way of:

- a decree (a court order) against the debtor for the debt; or
- a summary warrant, for debts such as council tax, income tax, value-added tax and National Insurance.

The most widely used diligence procedures are:

- *attachment* – which involves the seizing of a debtor's moveable property (e.g., money or goods) in pursuit of a debt;
- *arrestment* – which concerns a debtor's moveable property that is in the hands of another third party; and
- *inhibition* – which concerns immoveable property (e.g., land and buildings).

Several amendments to the law in this area have been made by the Bankruptcy and Diligence etc. (Scotland) Act 2007 and the Debtors (Scotland) Act 1987, both of which largely govern compensation and payments of debts due to creditors in Scotland today.

## Diligence on the dependence

Diligence means 'the process by which a person's lands or effects are seized for debts'. In this context, the term 'earnings' is interpreted liberally and includes the normal wages or salary of the debtor, as well as any fees, bonuses, commissions, pensions and annuities for previous services, statutory sick pay and compensation for loss of earnings that they receive. Diligence on the dependence is a provisional or protective measure which is used whilst a court action is ongoing, or just before an action is raised, but has not been finally disposed. It allows the creditor (pursuer) in the action to take steps to preserve the debtor's (defender's) property so that it will be available to satisfy any claim eventually upheld by the court.

An application is made to the court, but grounds must be established as to why the application is being made (i.e., the risk of flight, or disposal of assets by the debtor).

## Attachment

'Attachment', as defined in Part 2, s. 10(1) of the Debt Arrangement and Attachment (Scotland) Act 2002, is another form of diligence that allows a creditor to seize a debtor's *moveable property* as a means of recovering money owed (e.g., a vehicle for which the debtor is liable for payments).

Unlike arrestment, which is used against a debtor's property held by a third party, attachment is used to seize property owned by the debtor and in their possession. Attachment cannot be used to seize goods in the debtor's home unless an *exceptional attachment order* has been granted by a sheriff (see below). The creditor must have a decree (or relevant 'Document of Debt') and first have issued the debtor with a 'Charge for Payment', which must have expired, before proceeding with attachment. Where the debtor is an individual, the creditor must also have provided them with a Debt Advice and Information Package (DAIP).

Certain items cannot be attached under s. 11 of the Debt Arrangement and Attachment (Scotland) Act 2002. These include tools of a debtor's trade; books and artefacts needed by them for their profession; any vehicles the use of which is reasonably required by them and does not exceed a specified value; and mobile homes used as their main residence.

## Sheriff officers

At this juncture it is useful to introduce 'sheriff officers'. Sheriff officers are officers of the court in Scotland. They are either employed by private firms of sheriff officers or are self-employed. They accept instructions from individuals, companies, solicitors, local authorities and government departments. Sheriff officers enforce a variety of court orders, such as those concerning debt.

The court officers for the Court of Session are called 'messengers-at-arms' and have powers to enforce orders from the Court of Session. A messenger-at-arms is always also a sheriff officer.

## Procedure for attachment

A successful attachment thwarts a debtor moving attached articles from the place at which they were attached. It involves a sheriff officer attending to value, or arrange for the valuation of, the articles to be attached and then making a report of the attachment to the sheriff. After this has been received by the sheriff, under s. 15(1–3) of the of the Debt Arrangement and Attachment (Scotland) Act 2002, the sheriff officer may then remove and arrange for the sale of the attached articles.

Previously, certain public creditors pursuing debt by summary warrant were not required to serve a 'charge for payment' before executing attachment and proceeding to sell the attached articles. An amendment to s. 10 of the 2002 Act commenced on 1 April 2008, now making it necessary for public bodies to serve a charge for payment following summary warrant prior to attachment.

## Interim attachment

Interim attachment, as the name suggests, is a *provisional* diligence found under Part 1A of the of the Debt Arrangement and Attachment (Scotland) Act 2002. It protects the interests of creditors whilst their court action progresses, thus restricting the debtor's ability to deal with attached moveable assets in their possession pending its outcome. Interim attachment does not allow the creditor to remove or sell the attached items. The court may, however, upon application any time after interim attachment, make provision for the security of attached articles. The scope of interim attachment is limited and excludes articles specified in s. 11 of the Debt Arrangement and Attachment (Scotland) Act 2002, as listed above.

As with diligence on the dependence, prior to a warrant for interim attachment being granted, a date must be set for a hearing. This gives the debtor, and any other person with an interest, the opportunity to make representation. In most instances, this hearing will be held prior to a warrant being granted. Where the court is satisfied that the creditor has a good case in the main action, or that there is a real risk that the creditor could be prejudiced in some way prior to the action being decided, then a warrant can be granted prior to the hearing. When a decree is granted, a further valuation and attachment by sheriff officers must be carried out before the creditor can proceed to sell attached goods.

## Exceptional attachment orders

Under s. 47 of the Debt Arrangement and Attachment (Scotland) Act 2002, an exceptional attachment order (EAO) authorises the attachment, removal and auction of non-essential assets belonging to the debtor and kept in a dwelling house.

Before granting an EAO, and as directed by s. 47(4)(a–h) of the Act, the sheriff will take several matters into consideration. These include the nature of the debt, whether the debtor resides in the dwelling house, whether they have had money advice (e.g., DAIP) and whether there is, or has been, any agreement between the debtor and creditor for the payment of the debt. The sheriff will also satisfy themselves that the creditor has taken reasonable steps to negotiate a settlement of the debt with the debtor. They will also check that the creditor has already executed or has attempted to execute an arrestment and an earnings arrestment and that there is a reasonable prospect that any sums recovered through exceptional attachment would produce the aggregate of chargeable expenses and £100 (s. 48(1)(2)).

Unlike ordinary attachment, articles attached under authority of an exceptional attachment order are removed immediately from the dwelling house unless it is impractical to do so. Once removed, attached articles may not be auctioned before seven days have elapsed from the date of removal. During this seven-day period the debtor may apply to the sheriff for an order that will cease the attachment and return the attached articles to the debtor, if the sheriff considers this appropriate in the circumstances.

## Arrestment on the dependence

Arrestment is a process by which a creditor 'attaches' or seeks to freeze assets which belong to his or her debtor but are currently *in the possession of a third party* (e.g., money in a bank account, a car in a garage, or shares in a company), with the effect that neither the third party nor the debtor is thereafter permitted to dispose of them.

The creditor is known as the 'arrester'. The debtor is known as the 'common debtor', and the third-party bank or building society is known as the 'arrestee'. After arrestment, the assets must remain in the hands of the arrestee. The assets merely remain frozen at this time and, while this may inconvenience the common debtor, it will be of little initial comfort to the arrester for reasons explained below.

## Bank arrestment

A bank arrestment in Scotland is when a creditor relying on Part 10 of the Bankruptcy and Diligence etc. (Scotland) Act 2007 seeks to attach funds held in a debtor's bank account, with a view to having those funds later transferred to them to pay said debt (e.g., to the Department of Work and Pensions for overpayment of benefits, local authorities for council tax arrears and Her Majesty's Revenue and Customs (HMRC) for tax owed).

If funds held by a bank or any other financial institution are arrested, there is a minimum amount that is protected from the arrestment. This is known as the 'protected minimum balance' and only the balance above that sum can be arrested. The protected minimum balance for funds held by financial institutions from April 2019 is £529.90.

Bank arrestments are called 'actions of arrestment and furthcoming' and are a two-stage process.

## Actions of arrestment and furthcoming

The first stage in bank arrestment is when the funds are *attached* by a creditor, such as a local authority regarding a debtor's unpaid council tax. This means that the debtor's bank is instructed to freeze the debtor's funds. The second stage is known as 'furthcoming', which is when these funds are taken from the debtor's account and given to the creditor. A successful action of furthcoming obliges the common debtor to pay the debt directly to the arresting creditor.

Governed by Part 10 of the Bankruptcy and Diligence etc. (Scotland) Act 2007, furthcoming can occur in only two situations. The first is when the debtor signs a mandate authorising their bank to transfer money to the creditor, which can be at any point after the arrestment. The second is fourteen weeks after the arrestment when, providing that there have been no objections lodged by the debtor, the funds are transferred to the creditor without the debtor's agreement. Note *Stewart v Royal Bank of Scotland* (1994), which concluded that where a defender's account is held at an English branch of a bank, but the pursuer serves an arrestment on a Scottish branch of that bank, the arrestment will not 'catch' the defender's account.

## Earnings arrestment

Wage arrestment in pursuance of debt in Scotland is more properly known as an 'earnings arrestment'. An earnings arrestment sees the court grant an 'earnings arrestment order' under Schedule 2 of the Debtors (Scotland) Act 1987. For this to be granted, the creditor must first raise a charge for payment that must be notified to the debtor before an EAO can be granted. A 'charge for payment' is a legal document that is served in Scotland by sheriff officers. They are served to formally demand payment of money and give the debtor fourteen days to pay. If the charge is not complied with there are consequences in terms of an EAO then being awarded by the court.

It is important to note that for the arrestment order to be legitimate, the creditor must also arrange for a DAIP to be sent from the Accountant in Bankruptcy to their debtor, no less than twelve weeks before serving the order.

## Earnings arrestment orders

Non-compliance by a debtor to a charge for payment can see an earnings arrestment order being issued by the court under the Diligence Against

Earnings (Variation) (Scotland) Regulations 2018, that is served against them by sheriff officers under Schedule 2 of the Debtors (Scotland) Act 1987. This type of arrestment requires the debtor's employer to deduct sums in accordance with the earnings arrestment tables contained in s. 53 of the Debtors (Scotland) Act 1987, as do two other types of earnings arrestment: current maintenance arrestment; and conjoined arrestment orders.

### Current maintenance arrestment

Current maintenance arrestment can be used to enforce the payment of maintenance (e.g., a regular allowance awarded by a court on divorce) when the debtor is in default. To be effective the creditor must have a current maintenance order from the court on which the debtor has defaulted and, where the debtor is an individual, the creditor must also have provided them with a DAIP.

This type of arrestment requires the debtor's employer to deduct sums in accordance with the earnings arrestment tables at s. 53 of the Debtors (Scotland) Act 1987 and to then pass the deduction to the creditor.

### Conjoined arrestment order

A conjoined arrestment order is granted by the court to enforce payment of two or more of the same type of debt, at the same time. For conjoined arrestment orders, the debtor's employer is required to make a deduction, but this time pass it to the court to distribute the funds. The amount deducted remains the same as it would for a single arrestment, only the sum is divided on a pro-rata basis between the conjoined creditors.

As with all the above diligences, the DAIP must be served on the debtor no earlier than twelve weeks before the arrestment.

### Summary warrants

Mention should be made regarding the differing procedure for certain types of debt that are owed to local authorities and HMRC. These are recoverable by way of a 'summary warrant' granted by the Sheriff Court. A summary warrant does not require a court hearing like other types of order.

Once a summary warrant has been issued, HMRC and local authorities can then serve a charge for payment on the debtor, giving them fourteen days' notice to pay their debts in full. Once served with a charge for payment, if the debtor has not paid, local authorities can use certain types of formal debt recovery process to recover the debt (e.g., bank and earnings arrestment).

## Inhibition on the dependence

In contrast to arrestment and attachment, an 'inhibition' is used in relation to heritable property – usually land or buildings – rather than money or moveable property. Part 5 of the Bankruptcy and Diligence etc. (Scotland) Act 2007 makes provision for many aspects of inhibition previously dealt with by common law.

An inhibition – a form of personal diligence – is used against heritable property in the ownership of the defender rather than property which is owed to them by a third party. An inhibition affects all of the defender's heritable property regardless of the amount of the claim by the pursuer, except when it is limited by the court 'on the dependence' of an action, or where the decree is granted in respect of an obligation to perform a particular act (e.g., to transfer heritable property to someone else). An inhibition which is limited applies only to the property specified in the action or specified by the sheriff.

An inhibition prevents the defender from dealing with their property in a way that might prejudice the claim of the pursuer (e.g., by selling it and disposing of the proceeds, transferring it or granting a security over it). It has the effect of preventing the debtor from dealing with any property for a five-year period without the creditor's agreement. It does not give the creditor the right to deal with the property, but if the debtor wishes to sell or refinance the property, it gives the creditor the prospect of having the debt repaid.

If the debtor becomes bankrupt or enters a trust deed, the trustee can deal with the debtor's property even though an inhibition exists over it. In such circumstances, an inhibition does not grant any preference to the inhibiting creditor.

## Decree of inhibition

To initiate an 'inhibition' a creditor must first apply to the court for a decree or a 'document of debt' against someone. A schedule of inhibition must be served on the debtor and, if an individual and the action is in respect of debt, as with arrestment, the creditor must also provide them with a DAIP.

Following service of the schedule of inhibition, the inhibition takes effect from the day that it is registered in the Register of Inhibitions and Adjudications, as under s. 155 of the Titles to Land Consolidation (Scotland) Act 1868. The exception to this is where a prior 'notice of inhibition' has been registered. In which case, the effect of the inhibition is backdated to the date on which the schedule of inhibition was served. This exception applies only where that service is registered before the expiry of twenty-one days from the registration of the notice.

## Consequences of an inhibition

The consequences of an inhibition become evident if the owner/debtor wishes to sell their heritable property. If a buyer is interested, they must engage the services of a solicitor to proceed the transaction. The first thing a solicitor will do is check the Register of Inhibitions to ascertain whether the seller of the land or building has an inhibition registered against them. If they do, the solicitor would advise their client against purchase, as it would put the potential buyer's title to the property at risk. To be able to dispose of such inhibited property, the owner must come to an agreement with their creditor to pay the debt due. And do so.

## CRIMINAL COURTS

### Criminal jurisdiction

There are four courts that hold jurisdiction in Scottish criminal proceedings:

- the Justice of the Peace Court;
- the Sheriff Court;
- the Sheriff Appeal Court; and
- the High Court of Justiciary.

### *The Justice of the Peace Court*

At the base of the Scottish criminal court hierarchy is the Justice of the Peace Court. The office of Justice of the Peace dates to 1609 in Scotland.

In 2001 Sheriff John McInnes QC was commissioned by the Scottish Government to produce a report on Scottish summary criminal justice. Following his Summary Justice Review Committee's Report to Scottish Ministers in 2004, today's Justice of the Peace Courts were created under the resulting Criminal Proceedings etc. (Reform) (Scotland) Act 2007. These Justice of the Peace Courts replaced district courts, which had previously been the responsibility of Scotland's local authorities. A new body, the Scottish Courts and Tribunals Service, became responsible for the administration of Justice of the Peace Courts, which are now organised by sheriffdom rather than, as previously, by local authority area.

Justice of the Peace Courts handle the least serious of crimes (e.g., being drunk and incapable, road traffic offences, minor shoplifting and breach of the peace). Perhaps not unsurprisingly, Justice of the Peace Courts are presided over by 'justices of the peace' (JPs). Being a JP is an honorary position, generally held by someone who could be considered a pillar of the community. Scotland's 450 JPs are appointed for five-year renewable terms by the Justices of the Peace Advisory Committees for each sheriffdom, and to the standards of appointment set by the Judicial Appointments Board for Scotland. Under the Justices of the Peace (Training and Appraisal) (Scotland) Order 2016, JPs receive statutory training before being given the task of trying their peers for minor criminal offences. There are no juries in Justice of the Peace Courts. Thus, such courts are held under summary procedure (see below).

A JP sits alone or on a bench of three. Both fact and law are determined by the JP. In view of their limited legal knowledge, JPs are given in-court guidance on points of law by a legally qualified 'clerk of court'. The relatively low gravity of offences tried before the court is reflected in the limited sentencing power of the JP – 60 days' imprisonment or a maximum fine of £2,500. JPs can also find caution for good behaviour (in lieu of, or in addition to, such imposed imprisonment or fine) for any period not exceeding six months. A breach of which can see the accused back in court facing another fine or imprisonment. JPs also have a signing role in granting search warrants and emergency child protection orders.

The office of the JP is not without controversy. It has been contended that JPs tend to be drawn from a particular socio-demographic background (i.e., white, middle class, conservative), which renders them non-representative of the public that they serve (and perhaps this is a concern that could be voiced regarding the judiciary in general). Moreover, the way in which they are appointed has certainly in the past led to concerns regarding their compatibility with human rights, particularly under Article 6 of the ECHR (right to a fair trial) (see R. White, 'Article 6, *Starrs* v *Ruxton*, *Clancy* v *Caird*, and Justices of the Peace', 2001 SLT (News), p. 105).

## The Sheriff Court

Here we are referring to the same sheriffs and Sheriff Courts that were discussed earlier in this chapter regarding relevant civil cases. The Sheriff Court hears cases that pertain to crimes more serious than those heard in the Justice of the Peace Court. Examples would be theft, assault and possession of drugs.

There are two distinct court procedures which may be adopted. With less serious crimes and as with Justice of the Peace Courts, the 'summary procedure' will apply (readers should not confuse this term with 'summary cause' procedure in civil cases as discussed earlier), and in more serious criminal cases 'solemn procedure'.

## Summary procedure

In summary procedure, a sheriff will hear the case alone and must determine points of law relative to the case to then make a judgment based on the facts proved in court. The penalties that a sheriff sitting in summary proceedings may impose are a maximum fine of £10,000 and up to twelve months' imprisonment.

## Solemn procedure

In respect of more serious offences, solemn procedure is appropriate. Here, the legal issues are determined by a sheriff, but crucially the facts of the case are determined by a jury consisting of fifteen members of the public. It is the jury that determines guilt based on said facts. Reflecting the higher gravity of offences alleged, under solemn procedure, if the jury find the accused guilty, the sheriff may impose an unlimited fine and a term of imprisonment of up to five years. In cases in which it is felt that these sanctions would not represent an adequate punishment, the sheriff may remit the case to the High Court of Justiciary, which may issue a harsher penalty.

## High Court of Justiciary

Developed from the old judicial office of Justiciar, the High Court of Justiciary was established in 1672 and is the supreme criminal court in Scotland. Although traditionally the High Court was based in Edinburgh, it now travels 'on circuit' to cities throughout Scotland as required, albeit with a permanent sitting in Edinburgh and Glasgow. The same judges sit in the High Court as preside over the Court of Session. The court consists of the Lord President (termed 'Lord Justice-General' when acting in this criminal capacity), the Lord Justice-Clerk, and all the other Court of Session judges (called 'Lords Commissioners of Justiciary' in this context). The most serious of crimes are tried in the High Court of Justiciary, including murder, culpable homicide, serious sexual offences, armed robbery and drug trafficking. Reflecting the extreme gravity of such offences that are tried before the court, High Court judges hold an unlimited sentencing power, except that in some circumstance's sentences are imposed by Parliament (e.g., life imprisonment for a murder conviction).

In the High Court of Justiciary a single judge presides over criminal trials to determine legal issues and, similar to solemn procedure in the Sheriff Court, with a jury of fifteen present who are responsible for deciding upon the facts of the case. Very occasionally, benches of three judges preside over particularly important or complex cases.

## Scottish Court in the Netherlands

A famous example here would be when between May 2000 and March 2002 the High Court of Justiciary sat as the Scottish Court in the Netherlands to try Libyan's Abdelbaset al-Megrahi and Lamin Khalifah Fhimah for the bombing of Pan Am Flight 103 over Lockerbie, Scotland on 21 December 1988. Presiding Judge Lord Sutherland assisted by Lords Coulsfield and MacLean found Fhimah not guilty and he returned to Libya, while Al-Megrahi was found guilty and convicted for the murders of Pam Am 103's 259 passengers and crew and eleven Lockerbie residents. His appeal against the conviction was held at Camp Zeist in the Netherlands by five Scottish judges but was rejected. He went on to serve eight years of a life sentence before being returned on compassionate grounds in 2009 to Tripoli in Libya where her died three years later of terminal cancer.

## Appeals in the High Court of Justiciary

The High Court of Justiciary is also an appeal court, with cases referred to it by its own trials, and, with its permission, cases from the Sheriff Appeal Court. Appeals are heard in the High Court buildings in Edinburgh by a panel of two judges against sentence, and three judges against conviction – although in cases of high societal import, a panel of five or more judges may sit. A notable case heard by a full bench involved a re-casting of rape laws in Scotland (Lord Advocate's Reference (No. 1 of 2001) (2002)).

There are two categories of appeal: summary appeals; and solemn appeals.

### Summary appeals

Summary appeals (by way of the 'justiciary roll') are generally brought under the 'stated case' procedure. An appeal may be brought by the defence against conviction, sentence, or both. Further, the appellant may bring fresh evidence, but in general all appeals are made on a point of law.

The prosecutor in summary procedure may appeal, but only on a legal point which has led to an acquittal. Moreover, if some procedural irregularity is being alleged, either party may bring an appeal on such grounds, by virtue of a 'bill of suspension' (by the accused) or 'bill of advocation' (by the prosecutor).

In an appeal, the court may order a retrial or an acquittal; confirm the original verdict; or reduce or increase the sentence (if the appeal related to sentence).

## Solemn appeals

With solemn appeals (on the 'criminal appeal roll') the accused may appeal against sentence and/or conviction. The rights of appeal as to irregularity in court procedure, that arise in respect of summary appeals, may also be exercised by prosecutor and defence. The defence may again appeal on the facts only if fresh evidence is brought to the court. The prosecutor may appeal against the sentence if they are of the opinion that a harsher sentence better fits the crime. The Lord Advocate may also raise an appeal on a point of law if the accused has been acquitted.

Whatever the outcome of this appeal, however, the acquittal of the accused will not be overturned.

## Scottish Criminal Cases Review Commission

Under s. 25 of the Crime and Punishment (Scotland) Act 1997, the Scottish Criminal Cases Review Commission (SCCRC) – an independent body comprising members of the legal profession and other relevantly qualified individuals – may remit a case to the High Court for review if it is felt that this is in the interests of justice. This power may be exercised by the SCCRC regardless of the result of any appeals that have already been held, as in the case of Abdelbaset Ali Mohmed al-Megrahi (see above). In 2007, the SCCRC granted al-Megrahi leave to appeal for a second time. Al-Megrahi, however, withdrew this second appeal two days before the Scottish Government announced on 20 August 2009 that he was to be released on compassionate grounds and returned to Libya. He later died of prostate cancer at his villa in Tripoli on 20 May 2012. Since his death, his family have agitated for a posthumous appeal. This was granted by the SCCRC in May 2020 after considering six grounds of review, concluding that a miscarriage of justice may have occurred by reason of 'unreasonable verdict' and non-disclosure'.[1]

---

[1] SCCR news release, 11 March 2020, application on behalf of Mr Abdelbaset Ali Mohmed Al Megrahi, <https://irp-cdn.multiscreensite.com/8f56052e/files/uploaded/11%20March%202020 %20-%20SCCRC%20News%20Release%20-%20Application%20on%20behalf%20of%20 Mr%20Abdelbaset%20Ali%20Mohmed%20Al%20Megrahi_dgMrLN20RqqEoEwzK4eV.pdf>.

Consequently, the case has been referred back to the High Court of Justiciary. (For further examples of the SCCRC's work, see: www.sccrc.org.uk)

## Appeals to the Supreme Court

The functions of the Judicial Committee of the House of Lords were transferred to the Supreme Court with effect from 1 October 2009. But there still exists a further right of appeal in certain Scottish criminal matters to the now Supreme Court. Such an appeal is by way of 'devolution minute' only. This right relates to situations (among others) where it is contended that the Scottish courts have gone beyond the powers delegated to them by the Westminster Parliament under the Scotland Act 1998. In *HM Advocate* v *H* (2002), the accused lodged a devolution minute following an amendment of the definition of 'rape', which occurred in a decision of the High Court of Justiciary in *Lord Advocate's Reference* (No. 1) of 2001 (2002). H argued that, in formulating a new law, the court had breached the concept of the separation of powers and had violated human rights considerations. Lord McLean, however, held that the High Court had merely corrected the law and the appeal was unsuccessful.

### *Cadder* v *HM Advocate*

Cadder appealed to the Supreme Court in 2010. In effect, his appeal was against an earlier ruling by the High Court of Justiciary in *HM Advocate* v *McLean* (2009). In *McLean* the High Court of Justiciary held that reliance by the Crown on admissions made by an accused who had not had access to a solicitor while detained under s. 14 of the Criminal (Procedure) Scotland Act 1995 *did not* violate Article 6(1) and 6(3) of the ECHR. Article 6(1) concerns an accused's right to a fair trial, while Article 6(3) guarantees, among other things, an accused's right to free legal assistance.

Cadder himself had been detained by the Police under s. 14 of the Criminal (Procedure) Scotland Act (1995). In the police station he declined the offer that a solicitor be contacted on his behalf. Consequently, he did not have the benefit of legal representation or advice before, during or after his s. 14 interview, during which he made several admissions. These were later led by, and relied upon, by the Crown in court, which resulted in his conviction. On 26 October 2010, the Supreme Court, relying on the European Court of Human Rights decision in *Salduz* v *Turkey* (1998), held that the law and practice of police interviewing such detained persons as *Cadder* in a police station without allowing them access to legal advice *was* against Article 6(1) and 6(3) of the ECHR. Further, that the Crown *thereafter* leading evidence obtained in such circumstances was in breach of s. 57(2) of the

Scotland Act (1998); which prevents members of the Scottish Government (in this case the Lord Advocate) from acting incompatibly with Convention rights or EC law. Crucially, the Supreme Court in *Cadder* emphasised that its decision could not be applied retrospectively. This could have seen thousands of similar appeals against conviction.

The immediate response of the Scottish Government was to pass the Criminal Procedure (Legal Assistance, Detention and Appeals) (Scotland) Act 2010 under emergency legislation procedure that came into force in October of the same year.

## The Carloway Review

Following *Cadder*, in November 2010 Holyrood Cabinet Secretary for Justice Kenny MacAskill established the 'Independent Review of Law and Practice' under the chairmanship of Lord Carloway; then a senior High Court judge, who over the following year considered a range of aspects of Scottish criminal law and practice. His Lordship is currently Lord President of the Court of Session and Lord Justice General, the most senior judge of the Supreme Courts of Scotland and head of the Scottish Judiciary.

Carloway reported back in November 2011. His terms of reference were to consider issues relating to the right of access to legal advice, police questioning, detention and evidence. Describing several of his own recommendations as 'radical and substantial', their purpose is to ensure Scotland's criminal justice system complies with the ECHR in law, practice and attitude. Carloway recommended:

- a person's right to legal advice when taken into custody;
- limiting the period of a person's arrest before charge to twelve hours;
- introducing protection and rights for children and vulnerable adults;
- giving greater powers to the police to conduct structured investigations;
- less restrictive rules around evidence and abolishing the need for corroboration; and
- adjusting the relationship between the SCCRC and the High Court.

A great deal of the Review met with acclaim. However, the recommendation to abolish the need for corroboration of evidence in criminal trials immediately caused controversy. Encouraged by Carloway and lobbied by

Police Scotland and the Crown Office and Procurator Fiscal Service, the Scottish Government attempted to pass this reform by way of the Criminal Justice (Scotland) Bill 2013. The proposal to no longer require the need for corroboration was, however, abandoned after strong opposition from the Law Society for Scotland, and the Faculty of Advocates. And, as a result, was not included in the later Criminal Justice (Scotland) Act 2016 that passed most of Carloway into law.

Notwithstanding, *Cadder* continued to cause controversy. In May 2011, Nat Fraser successfully appealed to the Supreme Court against his conviction and life sentence in 2003 for the murder of his wife Arlene in Elgin. He also relied on Article 6(1) of the ECHR. This saw the Court of Criminal Appeal in Edinburgh formally quash his conviction in June 2011 and order a retrial. His liberty was, however, short-lived in that at this subsequent trial he was again found guilty and sentenced to a further seventeen years' imprisonment.

The Fraser case prompted an unprecedented political backlash involving Scotland's then First Minister Alex Salmond and his Justice Secretary Kenny MacAskill, both questioning the right of the UK Supreme Court to have an appeal function in Scottish criminal cases. This led to a review group being set up under the chairmanship of Lord McCluskey to examine the relationship between the High Court of Justiciary and the UK Supreme Court in criminal cases. The group reported in late 2011, recommending that the UK Supreme Court *should* continue to have the power to rule on human rights issues that arise from Scottish criminal law cases, but only if the High Court of Justiciary permits the appeal. Permission would be granted through a certificate noting the case raises a point of public importance.

## CRIMINAL PROCEDURE

Any detailed exposition of Scottish criminal court procedure is beyond the scope of this book, but the following short discussion should help identify some of its main procedural aspects.

### Criminal investigation

While Police Scotland carry out investigations into the commission of crime, decisions regarding any subsequent prosecution are taken by the Procurator Fiscal (PF), who acts on reports received by the police. The PF is the local representative of the Lord Advocate (Head of the Crown Office and Procurator Fiscal Service (COPFS), currently James Woolfe QC).

Depending on the gravity of the alleged offence, a decision will be taken by the PF as to which court the case will be tried in (and, if in the Sheriff Court, whether the procedure should be *solemn* or *summary*). The PF may alternatively decide that it is not in the public interest for a prosecution to proceed. It should be noted that prosecution is *almost* always brought by the state through the PF.

## Private prosecutions

Although private prosecutions are commonplace south of the border, under s. 6 of the Prosecution of Offences Act 1985, private prosecutions in Scotland are allowed but are very uncommon. This is partly due to the onerous process of instigating such an action. To bring a private prosecution, an individual must apply to the High Court for a 'Bill for Criminal Letters', which can be opposed by the Lord Advocate and the alleged offender. There must also be *special circumstances* to justify a private prosecution, which can be very difficult to establish.

One of the most recent but ultimately unsuccessful applications to the High Court for a Bill for Criminal Letters occurred in 2016 following the 'Glasgow Bin Lorry' tragedy of 22 December 2014. On that day, Harry Clarke, a Glasgow City Council refuse truck driver lost consciousness at the wheel of his lorry crossing George Square in central Glasgow. The truck then mounted the pavement killing six people and injuring seventeen others before crashing into the Queen Street Railway Station underpass and then coming to a halt. After the COPFS announced on 25 February 2015 that there would be no criminal charges forthcoming against Mr Clarke, evidence was averred by relatives of three of the deceased that Mr Clarke had failed to declare his previous medical history of 'blackouts' to his employers Glasgow City Council and also to the Driver and Vehicle Licensing Agency which had issued his driving licence. Consequently, representatives of the Sweeney/McQuade families raised an action for a Bill for Criminal Letters at the High Court in January 2016, seeking authority to privately prosecute Mr Clarke under ss. 1, 1A and 2 of the Road Traffic Act 1988; or alternatively for the common law offence of culpably and recklessly driving the vehicle on the date in question and causing the deaths of the pedestrians. The High Court, however, concluded that: 'even if we had disagreed with the Crown's assessment, or the weight attributed to individual pieces of evidence, we would be unable to conclude that the decision of the Lord Advocate not to prosecute was so extravagantly wrong as to amount to special circumstances justifying the passing of the bills in either case.' (For further information, see www.scotcourts.gov.uk/search-judgments/judgment?id=d26a25a7-8980-69d2-b500-ff0000d74aa7

## Procedure in solemn cases

Solemn case court process begins life with a petition at the instance of the PF. The accused may be arrested because of a warrant in the petition, although they may already have been arrested prior to the petition being served.

The first appearance of the accused in the court process is always before a sheriff in the Sheriff Court, even if the case is ultimately to be determined before the High Court of Justiciary. This first hearing is termed a 'first examination' and takes place in private. Nothing of any real substance occurs at this first hearing, and the accused will generally not enter any plea or declaration at this time. The PF will move for 'committal' either for trial or for further examination. The accused will be kept in custody at this point unless bail is granted. At this stage the case preparation by the prosecution and defence will begin in earnest. For example, all police statements and any declaration by the accused are sent to the Crown Office, and all witnesses will be interviewed (or 'precognosced') by the PF. The Crown Office will then determine what charges the accused will face in court, which may in fact differ from those originally set out on the petition. The accused is then served with a document known as an 'indictment' that details the offences alleged, the time and place of the crime, a list of witnesses and a list of 'productions' (being documents to be used in evidence). Non-documentary productions (i.e., actual articles) are also listed and numbered separately. They are termed 'labelled productions' because of the labels attached to them, which describe the article and state where they were found. The labels are signed by the witnesses who will identify them at trial. Documentary productions are initialled by the witnesses who are to speak to them. The indictment will also set a date for trial.

Where the case is to be heard in the Sheriff Court there will be a 'first diet' prior to the trial. This diet is to ensure that the parties are sufficiently prepared to proceed to trial. Where the case is to proceed to the High Court of Justiciary, previously there was no provision for a first diet, but instead a 'preliminary diet' could be held if either party gave written notice to the court requesting such a hearing. A mandatory preliminary hearing was, however, introduced by the Criminal Procedure (Amendment) (Scotland) Act 2004. The High Court preliminary hearing, as well as a first diet in the Sheriff Court, may be used by the defence to deal with a number of preliminary issues prior to trial, such as a 'plea to the competency' of the court to deal with the offence or the relevance of the charge in that the allegations made by the Crown regarding the accused do not amount to an offence under Scots law.

An example of the latter concerns the case of Professor Clara Ponsati of St Andrews University. Ponsati is, at the time of writing, the subject of an extradition request by the Spanish Government, when, following her involvement as Catalan Minister for Education in the Generalitat of Catalonia in October 2017, she helped organise an independence referendum in the region. According to the Spanish Government, such a unilateral action by a devolved administration is illegal under the Spanish Constitution. The Spanish authorities subsequently charged her with the crime of sedition, which her solicitor Aamer Anwar argues does not exist in Scots law. This theoretically suggests extradition may be impossible. Alternatively, the COPFS, which is pursuing the case on behalf of the Spanish Government, intends arguing that Ponsati's conduct constitutes the offence of treason under the law of Scotland. A full trial was scheduled for Spring 2020 but is currently suspended.[2]

A 'plea in bar of trial' may also be made at a first diet. This relates to the lodging of one of four special defences by the defence: namely, insanity; alibi; incrimination (the blaming of another named party); or self-defence.

In both the Sheriff Court and the High Court of Justiciary, the next stage of the procedure is the trial. There are strict time limits within which a case must be brought to trial when an accused is in custody. It was a well-established rule that an accused in custody must be served with an indictment within eighty days. A further rule prescribed that the trial had to take place within 110 days of the accused being taken into custody. Where these time limits were not adhered to, accused persons had then to be set free and were immune to further prosecution. These consequences were a way to ensure fair treatment of accused persons; in particular, that the state was not empowered to lock up individuals for lengthy periods without bringing them forward for trial.

However, much to the disquiet of libertarians, under the Criminal Procedure (Amendment) (Scotland) Act 2004 the situation has been altered quite radically. The eighty-day rule concerning the serving of

[2] 'Catalonia: Scots sheriff postpones ruling on Ponsati extradition', The National, 6 March 2020, <www.thenational.scot/news/18284773.catalonia-scots-sheriff-postpones-ruling-ponsati-extradition/>.

an indictment still stands, but the Crown now has 140 days to bring an accused in custody to trial. More importantly, where the limits are not adhered to, the accused is liable to be given bail, but the charges may still be taken forward and they may be brought to trial later. Where the accused is not in custody while awaiting trial, the preliminary hearing must take place within eleven months of the first examination.

The Criminal Justice and Licensing (Scotland) Act was passed by the Scottish Parliament on 30 June 2010. The Act is wide ranging. Of note, and regarding criminal proceedings, are the provisions contained in Part 6 that came into force in June 2011. Part 6 provides a statutory framework for the Crown's duties in relation to the disclosure of evidence and, separately, imposes a duty on the defence to lodge defence statements in solemn cases, and an option to lodge the same in summary proceedings. While initiated quite some time ago, of recent significance to procedure in solemn cases in Scotland's criminal courts is the Bowen Review.

## The Bowen Review

In April 2009, the Scottish Government announced an independent review of sheriff and jury procedure in Scotland to:

> review the arrangements for sheriff and jury business, including the procedures and practices of the Sheriff Court and the rules of criminal procedure as they apply to solemn business in the Sheriff Court; and to make recommendations for the more efficient and cost-effective operation of sheriff and jury business in promoting the interests of justice and reducing inconvenience and stress to the victims and witnesses involved in cases.

The Review was undertaken by Sheriff Principal Bowen, who submitted his report to Scottish Ministers in June 2010. His 'Independent Review of Sheriff and Jury Procedure'[3] made several recommendations[4] including:

- to cite witnesses to give evidence in a case only once it is known that the case will proceed to trial;
- to introduce a 'new compulsory business meeting' to bring together the Crown and defence to discuss cases at an early stage of proceedings;

---

[3] Independent Review of Sheriff and Jury Procedure, <www2.gov.scot/Publications/ 2010/06/10093251/0>.
[4] Ibid.

- to enhance the current statutory provisions and require the Crown and defence at first diet to be able to inform the court about their preparation of the case and allow the court to resolve any issues to be addressed at that stage; and

- to allow a longer period between the indictment of the case and the first diet.

To accommodate these changes Sheriff Principal Bowen proposed that the statutory time limits for commencing trials in sheriff and jury cases be extended for custody cases to 140 days, in line with the High Court time limit. The Report also suggested that legal aid provision for sheriff and jury cases should be reviewed so that it supports early resolution of cases, as in the High Court and in summary justice.

Further recommendations were also made including the establishment of a working party to consider the wider use of TV links between courts and prisons; that the sheriffs should make greater use of existing powers relating to absentee jurors without excuse; and also that there should be continuity of sheriffs involved in individual cases. After a Public Consultation on the Review in 2012[5] much was accepted by the Scottish government and included in the Criminal Justice (Scotland) Bill 2013. A Bill that as a result of controversy (see subheading 'Corroboration' earlier in this chapter) did not become law until 2016. (For further information on procedure in solemn cases, see: www.gov.scot/publications/thematic-review-investigation-prosecution-sheriff-solemn-cases/)

## Procedure in summary cases

In summary cases, the prosecution normally starts by means of a document termed a 'complaint'. The complaint details the alleged offence, the name and address of the accused and the court that the accused must attend at a given date and time. The accused will normally then appear at a 'first hearing', during which they will be asked to tender a plea of 'guilty' or 'not guilty'. If the accused pleads guilty at this stage, sentence may be issued there and then. In respect of minor crime, which would not generally be punishable by a prison sentence, the accused may plead guilty by a letter. Where the accused tenders a not-guilty plea at the first hearing, the case will then proceed to an 'intermediate diet', during which the accused will be asked whether they wish to continue with this plea.

---

[5] 'Reforming Scots Criminal Law and Practice: Reform of Sheriff and Jury Procedure', <www2.gov.scot/Publications/2013/06/6725/2>.

The intermediate diet is also used to confirm that both sides – prosecution and defence – are ready to proceed to trial. If the plea is changed by the accused at this point to one of guilty, sentence may be passed immediately, although the court has the option of deferring sentence for social background reports. If there is no change in the plea at the intermediate diet, and both sides are ready, the case will then proceed to trial.

## Bail in criminal proceedings

As alluded to above, in both summary and solemn procedure, an accused may apply for 'bail' (i.e., to be released from custody) pending trial. Despite common perception, save for a few exceptional circumstances, there is no money deposited in court in return for bail. A court, however, may impose a number of conditions, including that the accused:

- will appear at the designated time at every subsequent court hearing;
- will not commit any offence on bail;
- will not interfere with any witnesses or in any other way attempt to pervert the course of justice; and
- will make themselves available for identification parades or for any evidential samples to be taken.

The granting of bail is often a controversial issue. While a libertarian viewpoint leans in favour of bail on the basis that an accused person is innocent until the charges against them are proven otherwise in court, a more prevalent viewpoint in society holds that those accused of at least the more serious of crimes should be locked up prior to trial on the grounds of public safety. The starting point, however, in *any* case in our courts is that bail *should* be granted. Bail is, of course, not always forthcoming, particularly in the more heinous of alleged crimes, and the court will take this and several other factors into account in arriving at its decision. Such would include:

- where it is suspected that the accused may commit a further crime;
- where it is considered that the accused may abscond;
- where there is deemed to be a risk of interference by the accused with the course of justice; and
- to prevent public disorder.

Appeals against a bail decision may be made by both the prosecution and defence.

## Sanctions in the criminal courts

The traditional sanctions that can be imposed against offenders are fines and imprisonment (or, if aged between sixteen and twenty-one years, detention in a Young Offenders' Institution). Sentences may be reduced accordingly where there are mitigating circumstances surrounding the commission of the offence, where the offender has no previous criminal record, or where an early guilty plea has been tendered by the accused.

## Alternative sentencing options

In addition, over recent years, policymakers have taken more holistic views on the issue of sentencing offenders, which might consider other policy aims apart from punishment, such as rehabilitation, deterrence and restitution. For example, from February 2011, because of s. 14 of the Criminal Justice and Licensing (Scotland) Act 2010, alternative sentencing options include the following Community Payback Orders:

- unpaid work or other activity or requirement;
- offender supervision requirement;
- compensation requirement;
- programme requirement;
- mental health treatment requirement;
- drug treatment requirement;
- alcohol treatment requirement;
- residence requirement; and
- conduct requirement.

(For further details on Community Payback Orders, see Scottish Sentencing Council at: www.scottishsentencingcouncil.org.uk/about-sentencing/community-payback-orders/)

## COURTS OF SPECIAL JURISDICTION

A range of other courts in Scotland hold jurisdiction in certain specified situations. Some of the more important courts are outlined below.

## Scottish Land Court

The Scottish Land Court holds jurisdiction to resolve a range of farming disputes, including cases involving landlord and tenant, agricultural and crofting matters. The court is based in Edinburgh but holds hearings throughout Scotland. It has a Chair who has the same status as a Court of Session judge; a Deputy Chair, who is an advocate, and two Members of Court, who are experienced in farming and crofting matters.

The current Chair of the court is Lord Minginish, who was installed on Friday 17 October 2014, following the retirement of Lord McGhie, who had been Chair since 1996. The current Deputy Chair of the Court is Iain F Maclean, who took up office on 14 September 2015. The present agricultural Members of Court are John Smith, who was appointed in March 2006, and Tom Campbell, who joined the court in February 2016. The Gaelic-speaking member of the court, as required in terms of s. 1(5) of the Scottish Land Court Act 1993, is Lord Minginish.

It should be noted that despite its name, the Scottish Land Court has no universal jurisdiction to deal with *all* matters relating to land. In particular, the court has no jurisdiction to deal with the question of ownership and heritable title to land (which are dealt with by the Sheriff Court and the Court of Session), nor does it have any jurisdiction in relation to urban subjects. (For further details on the Scottish Land Court, see: www.scottish-land-court.org.uk/)

## Lands Valuation Appeal Court

This specialist court hears appeals from decisions of local valuation appeal committees. Appeals are heard by stated case on a point of law only and are generally presided over by three Court of Session judges. In, for example, *City Assessor for Glasgow City Council v Monti Marino (Glasgow) Limited* (2012), the City Assessor appealed against the earlier decision of the Glasgow Valuation Appeal Committee of 28 June 2011 on an appeal by the respondent, Marino, relating to the entry in the property Valuation Roll at the 2010 Revaluation for a unit at the Silverburn Shopping Centre in Glasgow. The City Assessor entered the subjects as a 'shop' at a net annual value/rateable value of £159,000. The respondent contended that the subjects should instead be entered as a 'café' or 'restaurant' at a rateable value of £87,000. The Glasgow Valuation Appeal Committee allowed the appeal and applied the respondent's valuation. The Lands Valuation Appeal Court refused the appeal from the City Assessor.

The court noted that it has long been established that lands and heritage are valued in their current state without regard to the potential for physical adaptation (providing that use is beneficial and is not subject to arbitrary restrictions). They also emphasised that whether the subjects should have been entered in the Valuation Roll as a shop or a café was a question of fact for the Glasgow Valuation Appeal Committee. At least five considerations pointed to the unit being a café or restaurant:

1. the layout of the premises with tables and chairs for diners and seats outside;

2. the extent of food-based spending at the premises by comparison with food outlets that are valued as shops;

3. the fact that only a minority of the trade was take-away;

4. the fact that food was prepared on the premises for service at the tables; and

5. the availability of customer toilets.

Consequently, the Lord Justice Clerk, Lord Hardie and Lord Hodge concluded the Glasgow Valuation Appeal Committee's decision to value the subjects as a café/restaurant rather than a shop was not unreasonable, and there was therefore no error in law. Also, with regard to the assessor's contention that the Committee should not have ignored the rental evidence of the zoned shops, the Lands Valuation Appeal Court said that the Committee was entitled to impose its valuation, which it considered to be supported by the evidence relating to other food outlets at the centre. Since the Committee regarded the subjects as a restaurant, it was entitled to reject the values taken by the assessor from shops in the mall.

## Church Courts

The Church of Scotland operates a range of courts including the Kirk Session, Presbytery, Synod and General Assembly. Given the Church of Scotland's denominational status within Scotland, its courts – which deal exclusively with membership issues – sit independently from the Scottish law courts with no right of appeal to the Court of Session (see *Logan v Presbytery of Dumbarton* (1995)).

The courts of all other church denominations in Scotland do not have such independence.

## Courts Martial

Established within the armed forces to handle internal military disciplinary issues, these are courts of UK-wide jurisdiction. A Courts Martial Appeal Court, consisting generally of three or five judges from the High Court of Justiciary, may hear appeals from the courts martial. A further right of appeal to the Supreme Court may arise in matters of public interest.

## Court of the Lord Lyon

Originating in the fourteenth century, the Court if the Lord Lyon is presided over by the Lord Lyon King of Arms and exercises jurisdiction over such issues as heraldry, coats of arms and the use of clan badges. The Court of the Lord Lyon has both a criminal and civil jurisdiction. It may resolve disputes, issue fines and imprison offending individuals and/or seize any items of heraldry whose use or possession is unauthorised. Court of the Lord Lyon decisions may be appealed to the Inner House of the Court of Session and thereafter to the Supreme Court.

### Essential Facts

- There are two principal types of Scottish court: civil courts; and criminal courts.
- Civil courts with jurisdiction in Scotland include the Sheriff Court, the Sheriff Appeals Court, the Court of Session and the Supreme Court.
- Sheriff Courts are presided over by sheriffs. There are three different civil procedures: simple; summary cause; and ordinary cause.
- The Court of Session is based in Edinburgh and is split into two houses: the Outer House; and the Inner House.
- The Outer House has a wide jurisdiction in civil matters throughout Scotland. Cases are heard by a 'Lord Ordinary', who generally sits alone.
- The Inner House is primarily an appeal court. Normally, a panel of three judges hears appeals from the Outer House and the Sheriff Courts.
- The Supreme Court is the final court of appeal in the United Kingdom for civil cases, human rights and devolution matters. It replaced the Judicial Committee of the House of Lords in late 2009. It comprises twelve justices, two of whom are, by convention, Scottish. At the time of writing, these are Lord Hodge and Lord Reed. Lord Reed was appointed President of the Supreme Court on 20 January 2020 following the retirement of Lady Hale who served in this capacity from 2017.
- The Scottish courts may refer any issue governed by EC law to the ECJ to issue a ruling.
- Civil court remedies include specific implement, interdict, damages and declarator.
- 'Diligence' refers to various procedures by which creditors can recover court debts through freezing (and at times selling) the property of their debtors.

- 'Different diligence' procedures include arrestment, attachment, diligence and inhibition.
- The criminal courts in Scotland are Justice of the Peace Courts, the Sheriff Courts, the Sheriff Appeals Court and the High Court of Justiciary.
- Justice of the Peace Courts represent the bottom rung of criminal judicial hearings in Scotland. Presided over by lay judges known as 'justices of the peace', these courts handle the most minor offences in society. Justice of the Peace Courts replaced district courts in late 2009.
- Sheriff Courts are next in the criminal hierarchy. One of two procedures will be employed: for less serious crime, summary procedure; for more serious crime, solemn procedure. In summary cases the sheriff sits alone; in solemn proceedings, the sheriff determines issues of law while a jury of fifteen members of the public determines the facts.
- The Sheriff Appeals Court was first established in 2015 to hear criminal appeals, on 1 September 2018 the Sheriff Appeal Court's jurisdiction was extended to hear civil appeals. Before that date civil appeals were heard either by the sheriff principal for each sheriffdom or by the Inner House of the Court of Session.
- At the top of the criminal court hierarchy is the High Court of Justiciary, which deals with the most serious of offences such as rape, murder and treason. Cases are heard by a single judge known as a 'Lord Commissioner of Justice' and a fifteen-member jury.
- The High Court is also an appeal court. A panel of at least three judges hears appeals from decisions of High Court trials and those of the Sheriff Courts and Justice of the Peace Courts.
- Appeals by devolution minute may only be heard in the UK Supreme Court regarding Scottish criminal matters.
- In summary criminal procedure, prosecution is commenced on 'complaint'. There will be a first hearing and an intermediate diet prior to trial.
- In solemn criminal cases, prosecution is commenced on 'indictment'. There will be a first examination and a preliminary hearing prior to trial.
- Several sentences can be passed down in the criminal courts, including imprisonment, fines, admonition and Community Payback Orders.

## Essential Cases

*Starrs* v *Ruxton* (2000): temporary sheriffs abolished; the control over temporary sheriffs' appointment exercised by the Lord Advocate (as head of the prosecution service) was deemed contrary to the right to a fair trial under Article 6 of the ECHR.

*Karl Construction* v *Palisade* (2002): an inhibition on the dependence (i.e., prior to a court decree or equivalent) may be incompatible with Article 1 of First Protocol of the ECHR (the right to peaceful enjoyment of possessions).

*HM Advocate* v *H* (2002): the accused appealed against the High Court of Justiciary's amendment of 'rape' definition in Lord Advocate's Reference (No. 1) of 2001 (2002) on the basis that the court had breached the concept of separation of power and human rights considerations; the appeal was unsuccessful.

*Cadder* v *HM Advocate* (2010): The Supreme Court held, having regard to the decision of the European Court of Human Rights in *Salduz* v *Turkey* (2008), that the Crown's reliance on admissions made by an accused who had no access to a lawyer while he was being questioned as a detainee at a police station was a violation of his rights under Article 6(3)(c), when read with Article 6(1) of the ECHR.

## Website resources

### Courts in Scotland

Shelter Scotland

https://scotland.shelter.org.uk/get_advice/advice_topics/ complaints_and_court_action/structure_of_the_scottish_legal_ system/courts_in_scotland

### Court structure in Scotland

Judiciary of Scotland

www.scotcourts.gov.uk/about-the-scottish-court-service/the- scottish-civil-courts-reform

### Courts, tribunals and justice organisations in Scotland

Scottish Courts and Tribunals

www.scotcourts.gov.uk/taking-action/civil-online-gateway/welcome2

### Scottish Civil Courts reform

Scottish Courts and Tribunals

www.scotcourts.gov.uk/about-the-scottish-court-service/the-scottish-civil-courts-reform

### Sheriff Court – Civil Procedure Rules

Bankruptcy Rules – 2016

Child Care and Maintenance Rules

Child Support Rules

Fatal Accident Inquiry Rules

Lay Representation for Non-Natural Persons Rules

Ordinary Cause Rules

Sheriff Court Adoption Rules

Simple Procedure Rules

Small Claim Rules

Summary Applications, Statutory Applications and Appeals etc. Rules

Summary Cause Rules

Taxation of Judicial Expenses Rules

www.scotcourts.gov.uk/rules-and-practice/rules-of-court/sheriff-court---civil-procedure-rules

### Court of Session Rules

Chapters 1–107

www.scotcourts.gov.uk/rules-and-practice/rules-of-court/court-of-session-rules

### The Supreme Court

History, decided cases, procedures and current cases

www.supremecourt.uk

### Court of Justice of the European Union (CJEU)

Institutions of the European Union: CJEU role, composition and work

https://europa.eu/european-union/about-eu/institutions-bodies/court-justice_en

**What is diligence?**

Scotland's Insolvency Service: Accountant in Bankruptcy

www.aib.gov.uk/debt/owed-money/what-diligence

**Criminal Courts in Scotland**

The High Court, the Sheriff Court, the Sheriff Appeal Court and the Justice of the Peace Court

www.scotcourts.gov.uk/taking-action/criminal

**Children's Hearings Scotland**

Scotland's Children's Panel

www.chscotland.gov.uk/the-childrens-hearings-system/scotlands-childrens-panel/

**Scottish courts and tribunals**

About Scotland's Tribunals

www.scotcourts.gov.uk/the-courts/the-tribunals/about-scottish-tribunals

**Citizens Advice Scotland**

Commissioners and ombudsmen

www.citizensadvice.org.uk/scotland/law-and-courts/civil-rights/complaints1/

## Video resources

**Scottish criminal justice system, Part 1**

Global Glasgow

https://youtu.be/4xaKAgx_Uw4

**Scottish Criminal Justice System, Part 2**

Global Glasgow

https://youtu.be/5M25TkpeJGs

**Scottish criminal justice system, Part 3**

Global Glasgow

https://youtu.be/u3lQpGWe4L8

**Scottish criminal justice system, Part 4**

Global Glasgow

https://youtu.be/OciowQKWMOM

**The criminal justice system (Eric McQueen, Scottish Court and Tribunal Service)**

Education Scotland

https://youtu.be/knHnDWcpN4c

**Handling disputes in Scotland: the Scottish court system and progress of a court action**

Sheppwed

https://youtu.be/wMA8Re8mwHg

**Handling disputes in Scotland: diligence, arrestment and insolvency procedures**

Sheppwed

https://youtu.be/buzq1bTzpMg

# 4 ALTERNATIVES TO THE COURT PROCESS

The current judicial system relating to both criminal proceedings and civil actions in Scotland has been subject to a barrage of criticism, primarily because pursuing or defending an action through the civil courts can often amount to an expensive, time-consuming, confusing, adversarial and uncertain outcome. The civil court process has been subject to relatively recent reforms designed to alleviate some of these difficulties. For example, from January 1994, the rules for the conduct of civil litigation in the Sheriff Courts were streamlined (Act of Sederunt (Sheriff Court Ordinary Cause Rules) 1993) and the commercial action rules in the Court of Session were reformed in 2004 (Court of Session Practice Note No. 6 of 2004). Case management, in which judges seek to take a more active control in the timetabling of different aspects of civil cases with a view to expediting cases in a speedier fashion through the litigation process, has also begun to be implemented. In addition, new judges have been added to the Court of Session to bolster judicial manpower and cut down on case backlogs. Overlaid on all of this are the Gill Reforms, as discussed in Chapter 3.

Criminal justice reform has also been high on the public and political agenda of late. In this sense, one recent reform to help the progress of criminal cases has been the imposition of a single system of administration, which should arguably streamline and simplify the criminal justice process. It might be contended, however, that tinkering with procedures cannot paper over all the cracks of the Scottish judicial system. In civil matters, for example, there may often be better ways of resolving many civil disputes. Consequently, both the state and private bodies offer (and at times the state compels) a range of alternatives to the civil court process. Moreover, in criminal matters, a range of alternative mechanisms to prosecution through the court process has been devised. While some alternatives to traditional court processes, such as children's hearings, tribunals and arbitration, are well established, others, such as mediation and 'drug courts', are relatively new and unproven.

## CHILDREN'S HEARING PANEL

The children's hearing panel system was established following the Social Work (Scotland) Act 1968 as a method by which children, generally under sixteen years old, who may be in need of compulsory measures of care, could be dealt with. Nationally administered since 2013 by Children's Panel Scotland, children's hearing panels are found in every local authority area throughout Scotland.

According to Children's Panel Scotland, there are currently 2,500 volunteer lay members, who in 2018–19 heard more than 31,500 cases. In any sitting of the panel, a chair and two other lay members (including both male and female participants) will hear the case. The current procedures for operation of the panel came into being by way of the Local Government etc. (Scotland) Act 1994 but have since been updated by the Children (Scotland) Act 1995 and the Children's Hearings (Scotland) Act 2011. In every local authority, the panel is headed up by a Principal Reporter, an official who is answerable to a public body known as the Scottish Children's Reporter Administration (SCRA). As a non-departmental public body, SCRA's board, although acting independently, is accountable to Scottish Ministers at Holyrood. The Reporter is responsible for the referral of cases to the panel.

The Children's Hearing is empowered merely to dispose of the case. This means that it does not arrive at any findings of guilt or determine questions of law or fact, but only decides what measures should be taken in respect of the child. These issues must first be referred to a sheriff for determination prior to forwarding the case to the panel.

The right to appeal a Children's Panel decision is found in s. 154 of the Children's Hearings (Scotland) Act 2011. An appeal to the sheriff can be made up to twenty-one days following said decision by the child themselves, a relevant person in relation to the child, and/or by a safeguarder appointed in relation to the child by virtue of s. 30 of this same Act. A right of appeal to the Sheriff Appeal Court on a point of law or procedural irregularity is available. A subsequent right of appeal also exists to the Inner House of the Court of Session.

In respect of allegations of serious criminal offences, a child may be subject to general prosecution procedures in either the Sheriff Court or the High Court of Justiciary, rather than being dealt with by the panel. In such cases, however, the panel may still be called upon for the provision of advice to the court or to determine how the matter should be disposed.

Despite its solid reputation, it has been argued that operation of the children's hearing panel may be contrary to the right to a fair trial enshrined in Article 6 of the European Convention on Human Rights (ECHR). The argument here is that breach of Article 6 may be triggered where the Principal Reporter both institutes proceedings against the child concerned and acts in an advisory fashion to the panel of lay members about how the case should be disposed (see Norrie (2000)).

The case of *S v Miller* (2001) also raised doubts about the compatibility of the children's hearing system with the ECHR. In *Miller* it was argued that, as legal aid was not available for children's hearings, this might be inconsistent with the child's right to a fair trial under Article 6. To meet such concerns, legally aided advice is available from a solicitor (if the client qualifies) when it is discovered that a referral is being made. Legal aid is not available for the hearing itself, but it may be granted for dealing with any subsequent appeal. (For a summary, see: www.slab.org.uk/guidance/availability-of-childrens-legal-aid/)

More recently in *ABC v Principal Reporter and Others* [2018], the fourteen-year-old petitioner, ABC, challenged decisions made about his contact with his seven-year-old sibling, DEF, at two Children's Hearings in September and December 2017. The two children lived together with their parents (and their other siblings) until June 2016 when they were accommodated with different foster carers in terms of measures included in compulsory supervision orders made by the Children's Hearing in respect of each of them. ABC, who was returned to the care of his parents in July 2017, sought to challenge decisions made by the Children's Hearing in September 2017 and December 2017 which made certain provisions in relation to the restriction of his contact with DEF. The challenge required consideration of the relevant provisions of the Children's Hearings (Scotland) Act 2011 concerning the definition of a 'relevant person' – someone who can attend and participate fully in Children's Hearings – and their compatibility or otherwise with the procedural requirements of the right to respect for private and family life in terms of Article 8 of the ECHR.

The court found the notion of a relevant person as laid down in s. 81(3) of the 2011 Act as unduly narrow. And, in taking a purposive approach to the interpretation of the legislation, decided that words were required to be read into the definition of a 'relevant person' to make it more compatible with Article 8 – these being:

> Any individual other than a relevant person who appears to the Reporter to have or recently have had significant involvement in the upbringing of the child *or persons whose established family life with the child may be interfered with by the hearing and whose rights require the procedural protection of being a relevant person.*

(Readers may also wish to read Professor Ken Norrie on 'Human Rights and the Children's Hearing System', available from the Law Society of Scotland, at: www.lawscot.org.uk/members/journal/issues/vol-45-issue-04/human-rights-and-the-childrens-hearing-system/)

## TRIBUNALS

The exponential rise in state intervention that has been seen in public life over recent years has given rise to a range of new dispute areas in regard to administrative matters. Given that it has been deemed impractical to attempt to resolve this multitude of case-types through the civil courts, a wide range of administrative tribunals have thus been established, their purpose being to facilitate the quick and inexpensive resolution of such disputes.

In Scotland there are currently three different types of tribunal:

- Scottish Tribunals that deal with *devolved* issues and have *specific Scottish jurisdiction* and structures and are supported administratively by the Scottish Courts and Tribunals Service (e.g., the Mental Health Tribunal for Scotland);

- tribunals that deal with *reserved* issues but have *specific Scottish jurisdiction* and structures (e.g., the tribunal that deals with war pensions); and

- tribunals that deal with *reserved* issues and have *UK-wide jurisdiction* and structures (e.g., immigration and, until at least 2022, employment).

### Scottish Tribunals

In 2014 the Tribunals (Scotland) Act generated a new, simplified statutory framework for tribunals in Scotland, bringing together existing jurisdictions and providing a structure for new ones. The Act created two new tribunals: the First-tier Tribunal for Scotland; and the Upper Tribunal for Scotland.

The Lord President of the Court of Session, currently Lord Carolway, is the head of Scottish Tribunals and has delegated various functions regards these to the President of Scottish Tribunals, the Rt. Hon Lady Smith, herself a Judge at the Court of Session.

Table 4.1   Structure of Scottish Tribunals

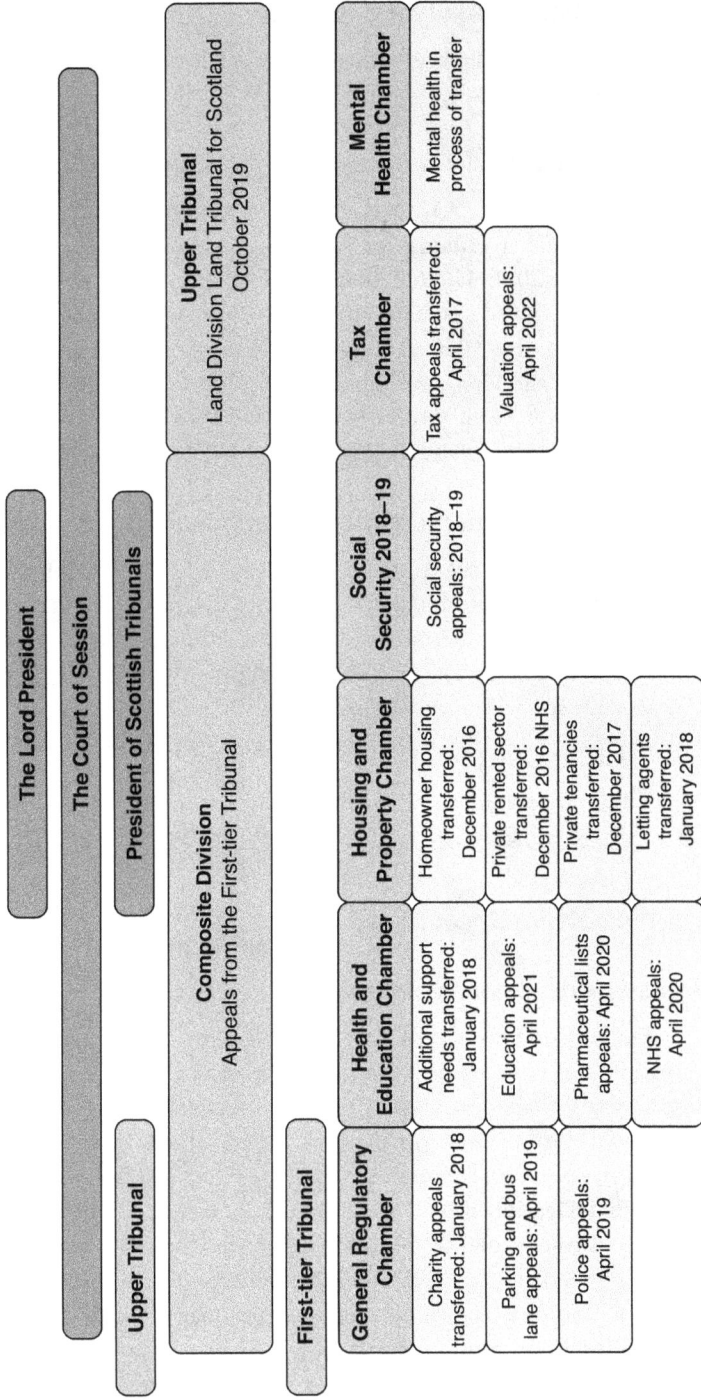

| The Lord President |
| --- |

| The Court of Session |
| --- |

| President of Scottish Tribunals |
| --- |

**Upper Tribunal**

| Upper Tribunal |
| --- |
| Land Division Land Tribunal for Scotland October 2019 |

| Composite Division |
| --- |
| Appeals from the First-tier Tribunal |

**First-tier Tribunal**

| General Regulatory Chamber | Health and Education Chamber | Housing and Property Chamber | Social Security 2018–19 | Tax Chamber | Mental Health Chamber |
| --- | --- | --- | --- | --- | --- |
| Charity appeals transferred: January 2018 | Additional support needs transferred: January 2018 | Homeowner housing transferred: December 2016 | Social security appeals: 2018–19 | Tax appeals transferred: April 2017 | Mental health in process of transfer |
| Parking and bus lane appeals: April 2019 | Education appeals: April 2021 | Private rented sector transferred: December 2016 NHS | | Valuation appeals: April 2022 | |
| Police appeals: April 2019 | Pharmaceutical lists appeals: April 2020 | Private tenancies transferred: December 2017 | | | |
| | NHS appeals: April 2020 | Letting agents transferred: January 2018 | | | |

## The First-tier Tribunal for Scotland

The First-tier Tribunal is organised into a series of chambers which have specialist jurisdictions.

### General Regulatory Chamber (Charity Appeals)

As illustrated in Table 4.1, the General Regulatory Chamber is a Chamber of the First-tier Tribunal for Scotland. It was created by the Tribunals (Scotland) Act 2014. The functions of the Scottish Charity Appeals Panel were transferred on 12 January 2018 to the First-tier Tribunal for Scotland and allocated to the General Regulatory Chamber. The Charity Appeals jurisdiction of the First-tier Tribunal deals with appeals against decisions made by the Office of the Scottish Charity Regulator, the body which regulates charitable activity in Scotland.

### Health and Education Chamber (Additional Support Needs)

On 12 January 2018, the Additional Support Needs Tribunals for Scotland transferred into the Health and Education Chamber of the First-tier Tribunal for Scotland to become the Additional Support Needs jurisdiction within the Chamber. The Health and Education Chamber is developing four separate specialist jurisdictions:

- Additional Support Needs;
- Education Appeals Committees;
- the NHS National Appeal Panel for Entry to the Pharmaceutical Lists; and
- the NHS Tribunal for Scotland.

### Housing and Property Chamber

The Housing and Property Chamber was formed to deal with the determination of rent or repair issues in private-sector housing, and assistance in exercising a landlord's right of entry. It established relatively informal and flexible proceedings to help resolve issues that arise between home-owners and property factors.

From 1 December 2017 the Chamber began to consider more cases from the private-rental sector. Such applications coming about under the Housing (Scotland) Act 2014 with the transfer of said jurisdiction from the Sheriff Courts regarding non-criminal matters arising from regulated, Part VII and assured tenancies.

The Housing and Property Chamber receives applications for rent assessments, the drawing up of terms, evictions and other non-criminal matters arising from the Private Housing (Tenancies) (Scotland) Act 2016. From 31 January 2018 the Chamber also began considering cases arising from new letting agents' legislation pertinent to the Housing (Scotland) Act 2014.

## Social Security Chamber

The Social Security Chamber of the First-tier Tribunal for Scotland was set up on 22 November 2018 following the Social Security (Scotland) Act 2018. It deals with appeals arising from a re-determination decision by the Social Security Scotland Agency acting on behalf of Scottish Ministers.

## Tax Chamber

The Scotland Act 2012 provided the Scottish Parliament with powers to introduce devolved taxes on land transactions and on waste disposal to landfill, effective from 1 April 2015. A First-tier Tribunal for Scotland Tax Chamber has thus been established to decide appeals made by Revenue Scotland – the new body for devolved taxes – in relation to its collection of Lands and Buildings Transaction Tax and Scottish Landfill Tax in Scotland.

## The Upper Tribunal for Scotland

The Upper Tribunal, as established by the Tribunals (Scotland) Act 2014, hears appeals on decisions made by the above First-tier Tribunal chambers under the Upper Tribunal for Scotland (Rules of Procedure) Regulations 2016, and the Upper Tribunal for Scotland (Rules of Procedure) Amendment Regulations 2016.

The Upper Tribunal hears appeals from a First-tier Tribunal on a point of law only and only with the permission of the First-tier Tribunal or another tribunal that may have made the decision (e.g., the Pensions Appeals Tribunal). If permission to appeal is refused, the Upper Tribunal can still decide to accept the case. A recent example is *Gdula* v *First-tier Tribunal for Scotland Housing and Property Chamber* (2019), where the Upper Tribunal found the earlier First-tier Tribunal of December 2018 had not erred in law in refusing to grant to the appellant a repossession of property that they once had and consequently, under Rule 3(6)(a) of the Upper Tribunal for Scotland (Rules of Procedure) Regulations 2016, refused Gdula permission to appeal.

The Court of Session hears appeals from the Upper Tribunal but only on a point of law and with the permission of the Upper Tribunal. If permission is refused, the Court of Session can nevertheless decide to take the appeal. Complicated or controversial cases can go straight to the Upper Tribunal without first going to its relevant First-tier Tribunal, but this is rare.

## Scottish Courts and Tribunals Service

The following Tribunals are administered by the Scottish Courts and Tribunals Service.

### The Mental Health Tribunal for Scotland

The Mental Health Tribunal for Scotland was created on 5 October 2005 by virtue of s. 21 of the Mental Health (Care and Treatment) (Scotland) Act 2003. Its headquarters are in Hamilton and it also has staff who work throughout Scotland. The President of the Tribunal presides over the discharge of the Tribunal's functions – who, as of 12 October 2019, is Laura Dunlop QC.

The Tribunal discharges its functions through panels of three members: a legal member (who acts as Convener); a medical member; and a general member. The judicial arm of the Tribunal is supported in its functions by the Scottish Courts and Tribunals Service (SCTS). The primary role of the Tribunal is to consider and determine applications for compulsory treatment orders (CTOs) under the 2003 Act, and to operate in an appellate role to consider appeals against compulsory measures made under the same. The Tribunal also plays a monitoring role by periodic review of compulsory measures imposed on patients.

The Mental Health Tribunal, its scope, powers and operation is and has been influenced by a raft of legislation, the most important of late being the Mental Health (Scotland) Act 2015 which covers *inter alia*:

- required written information where a CTO is to be extended (s. 2);
- transfer to another hospital (s. 3);
- emergency detention in hospital (s. 4); and
- short-term detention in hospital (s. 5).

There is a right under the Mental Health (Care and Treatment) (Scotland) Act 2003 to appeal to the Sheriff Principal (with a further appeal right to the Court of Session) or, in restricted patient cases, direct to the Court of Session. Grounds for appeal are that:

- the Tribunal decision was based on an error of law;
- there has been a procedural impropriety in the conduct of any hearing by the Tribunal on the application;
- the Tribunal has acted unreasonably in the exercise of its discretion; and
- the Tribunal's decision was not supported by the facts found to be established by the Tribunal (s. 324 of the Mental Health (Care and Treatment) (Scotland) Act 2003).

Where a patient is subject to a CTO or a compulsion order, their appeal must be made within twenty-one days of the date on which the decision was intimated to the patient (Rule 2(6) of the Act of Sederunt (Summary Applications, Statutory Applications and Appeals etc. Rules) 1999 (SI 1999/929). Where the patient is a restricted patient (i.e., subject to a compulsion order and a restriction order), the period for appeal is set out in the Mental Health (Period for Appeal) (Scotland) (No. 2) Regulations 2005 (SSI 2005/441) and essentially specifies a twenty-one-day period, which is linked either to the date on which the party is informed of the decision, or where the party has requested a copy of the document containing a full statement of the facts found and the reasons for the decision, within seven days of being informed of the decision from the date of receipt of that document.

An example of a recent appeal would be *R v Mental Health Tribunal for Scotland* (2017). R was a long-time diagnosed schizophrenic under a CTO granted in 2009 that had, from time to time, been varied in its application. The treatment regime for R under the CTO included antipsychotic medication coupled with periods of 'secure and safe in-patient care and assessment of his mental health and treatment requirements', as well as treatment, support and supervision by medical staff in the community. On 24 February 2017 a variation to the CTO resulted in treatment reverting from care in the community to hospital-based treatment. Mr R accepted that decision at that time. On 10 April 2017 Mr R applied under s. 100 of the Mental Health (Care and Treatment) (Scotland) Act 2003 to the Mental Health Tribunal for Scotland for revocation of his CTO because he believed that it was then no longer necessary. Alternatively, he sought variation of the CTO allowing him to be released from hospital as suitable care could, in his opinion, be provided in the community. His application was refused by the Mental Health Tribunal on 7 June 2017. He appealed the decision under s. 324(2)(c) of the Mental Health (Care and Treatment) (Scotland) Act 2003 to the Sheriff Principal on the grounds that the Tribunal had been unreasonable in the exercise of its discretion in its decision not to grant the variation. The basis being that the Tribunal had not considered the views of Mr R and his mother. Sheriff Principal Lewis concluded that the Tribunal had not failed in its responsibility to consider such relevant material. The Tribunal's decision to continue with the care in the community and hospitalisation treatment options for Mr R was reasonable in the circumstances, and his appeal was refused.

The Mental Health Tribunal for Scotland is due to move into the First-tier Tribunal for Scotland. Upon this transfer, a Mental Health Chamber will be established and the Mental Health Tribunal for Scotland, as such, will be abolished. Following transfer, the President of the Mental Health Tribunal will become President of the Mental Health Chamber.

### The Council Tax Reduction Review Panel

Council tax in Scotland is a local authority tax on domestic property introduced throughout the United Kingdom in 1993 following the passing of the Local Government Finance Act 1992. Assessed by each local authority, the amount of council tax charged on each property is a calculation determined by the property's assigned valuation based on property value – from band A (the lowest) to band H (the highest). The council tax replaced the controversial 'community charge' (popularly known as the 'poll tax') that saw local authority tax being assessed on the number of adults over 18 living in a property regardless of its value.

The Council Tax Reduction Review Panel (CTRRP) is independent of the local authority. It is a legally trained panel that can conduct a further review of a refused council tax reduction (CTR) decision made by any local authority in Scotland. An appellant must first ask their local authority to review their initial council tax decision before they can seek a review from the CTRRP. Strict time limits apply at each stage. To apply for a review and CTR the individual should first write to their local authority within two months of the initial decision on the amount that the local authority assess should be paid. If the individual disagrees with the returned CTR review decision by the local authority, they have the right to appeal to the CTRRP. This must also be in writing and made within six weeks of the date of the local authority's response. If the local authority does not reply within two months of receipt of a review request, an individual may then directly apply to the CTRRP for an independent review.

## The Pensions Appeals Tribunal

The Pensions Appeal Tribunal in Scotland hear appeals from ex-servicemen or women who have had their claims for a war pension rejected by the Secretary of State for Defence. England, Wales and Northern Ireland have their own tribunal. The Pension Appeals Tribunals' jurisdiction covers Scotland and is independent from Veterans UK. Veterans UK is part of the Ministry of Defence and administers the armed forces pension schemes and compensation payments for those injured or bereaved through service.

The Pension Appeals Tribunal has been in its present form since 1943, although it has been in existence, as part of the Lord President of the Court of Session's responsibility, since the War Pensions Act 1919. It is headed by a president who is legally qualified and supported by a panel of part-time legal chairpersons, medical members and service members. The current president in Scotland is Marion Caldwell QC.

## The Lands Tribunal for Scotland

The Lands Tribunal for Scotland is a tribunal with jurisdiction over land and property in Scotland relating to title obligations, compulsory purchase and other private rights. More specifically it is concerned with:

- the discharge or variation of title conditions;
- tenants' rights to purchase their public-sector houses;
- disputed compensation for compulsory purchase of land or loss in value of land caused by public works;
- valuations for rating on non-domestic premises;
- appeals against the Keeper of the Registers of Scotland;
- appeals about valuation of land on pre-emptive purchase; and
- voluntary or joint references in which the tribunal acts as arbiter.

The tribunal was established under the Lands Tribunal Act 1949, which also created the separate Lands Tribunals for England and Wales, and Northern Ireland. The rules in respect of tribunal applications are set out in the Lands Tribunal for Scotland Rules 2003. Although the statutory basis of a Lands Tribunal for Scotland was contained in the Lands Tribunal Act 1949, the tribunal itself was not actually created until 1971, as it was considered that there was not enough work to be undertaken. The Conveyancing and Feudal Reform (Scotland) Act 1970 gave the Lands Tribunal new powers to discharge title conditions and prompted its actual establishment in March 1971.

The Lands Tribunal for Scotland works in much the same way as a court in that it receives applications in appropriate form from an applicant, then arranges for issue of an order inviting any other interested parties to submit written answers, being objections or representations to said application. The Lands Tribunal for Scotland also arranges orders guiding and controlling the procedures.

The tribunal has a president who has overall responsibility for the organisation of its work, and three members who have recognised expertise in the fields of law and surveying. The current president of the tribunal is the Hon. Lord Minginish, who is also Chair of the Scottish Land Court. The tribunal members are Ralph A. Smith QC, Andrew Oswald FRICS and Charles Craigie Marwick FRICS. The former is legally qualified, the latter two are chartered surveyors. The tribunal itself (i.e., the three members) conducts hearings to take evidence and submissions for the parties, and then gives a written decision on the case, based on the evidence put before it by the parties concerned.

## TRIBUNAL PROCEDURE

The composition and procedures of tribunals vary, but a range of common factors can generally be identified. In the main, tribunals are headed by a legally qualified chair, assisted in the hearing of cases by appropriately trained lay members (as illustrated above regarding the Lands Tribunal for Scotland). Tribunals are organised on a local basis and hearings are generally held in public. Tribunal procedures are, at least in theory, more informal and less legalistic and time-consuming than court procedures. However, in practice the procedures may mirror the court process and it is not uncommon for parties to tribunal hearings to be represented by lawyers.

Administrative tribunals were established on the recommendation of the *Franks Report* (Cmnd 218, 1957) by the Tribunals and Inquiries Act 1958. The rationale behind administrative tribunals was that they would be open, fair and impartial, and pay regard to notions of natural justice. To ensure that such aims are met, in November 2013 the interim Scottish Tribunals and Administrative Justice Advisory Committee was created by Scottish Ministers on the abolition of the Administrative Justice and Tribunals Council and its Scottish Committee.

The decisions of administrative tribunals can be challenged in two ways. First, a decision may be appealed either on the facts or on a point of law to an appeal tribunal, a court or a government minister. In addition, the decisions of administrative tribunals may be subject to the process of judicial review through the Court of Session. In general, judicial review is applicable where it is alleged that the tribunal concerned has acted out-with its powers (*ultra vires*) or contrary to the principles of natural justice. This remedy is normally available only where all other avenues of objection have been exhausted.

## EMPLOYMENT TRIBUNALS

A tribunal of some importance is the Employment Tribunal, primarily regulated under the Employment Tribunals (Constitution and Rules of Procedure) Regulations 2004. These tribunals can hear an array of employment disputes between employee and employer including sexual, racial and disability discrimination, equal pay and unfair dismissal. Such cases must be brought to the tribunal rather than the civil court.

The typology of cases considered by UK Employment Tribunals was recently extended in the case of Jordi Casamitjana who, in January 2020, claimed that he was unfairly sacked by the animal charity the League Against Cruel Sports after raising concerns with colleagues that its pension fund invested in companies involved in animal testing. His 'ethical veganism' was deemed by Employment Tribunal Judge Robin Postle to satisfy the tests necessary for ethical veganism to be held a philosophical belief under, and thus protected by, the Equality Act 2010. Following *Grainger plc v Nicholson* [2010], for a belief to be protected it must meet a number of tests that include being worthy of respect in a democratic society; not being incompatible with human dignity; and not being in conflict with the fundamental rights of others. At a later hearing on the lawfulness of Casamitjana's dismissal the LACS conceded his actions were 'genuine and correct' and agreed a settlement. Subsequently, the League Against Cruel Sports also changed its pension policy.[1]

A tribunal is chaired by a legally qualified party, normally assisted by two lay members, one drawn from each side of the trade union or employers' association divide. Tribunal panels are empowered to conduct proceedings in any manner that they deem most suitable and, in practice, the process tends to be relatively informal when compared to court processes. Decisions can be reviewed by an Employment Tribunal if:

- they were wrongly made as a result of an administrative error;
- the appellant did not receive notice of the proceedings leading to the decision;

---

[1] "Jordi Casamitjana vegan tribunal a 'victory for animal protection'." BBC News 2 March, 2020 <www.bbc.co.uk/news/uk-england-london-51709141>.

- the decision was made in the absence of either the appellant or the respondent (the person claimed against);
- new evidence has become available since the conclusion of the hearing; or
- a review is required in the interests of justice.

## Employment Tribunals and the Smith Commission

After the 2014 Scottish independence referendum the Westminster Government established a commission under the chairmanship of Lord Smith of Kelvin to give more powers to the Scottish Parliament. His report, known as the 'Smith Commission', later formed much of the Scotland Act 2016 that set out amendments to the Scotland Act of 1998 giving further devolved powers to Scotland. Among these devolved powers were aspects of employment law and the devolution to Scotland of the administration and oversight of previously reserved tribunals to now be under the aegis of the Scottish Courts and Tribunals Service – one such previously wholly reserved tribunal being the Employment Tribunal.

At the time of writing, concern is being raised by trade unions and employment law firms that, five years later, Employment Tribunals have still not yet transferred. And, according to the SCTS[2] in February 2020, are unlikely to do so until at least 2022.

## Employment Appeal Tribunal

The Employment Appeal Tribunal (EAT) may hear appeals from those 'awards' arrived at by Employment Tribunals. The EAT consists of a Court of Session judge aided by several other members with recognised skill and experience in the employment field. An appeal can only be heard by an EAT on a 'point of law', or how the law was interpreted and applied in the earlier instance. An example being that the judgment was one which no reasonable Employment Tribunal could have reached.

Appeal to an EAT is by way of a 'notice of appeal', and strict time limits apply – forty-two days after receipt of the written judgment of the Employment Tribunal. An additional right of appeal from the EAT may be brought to the Inner House of the Court of Session and again to the

---

[2] 'Concern over delay to Smith Commission's devolution of tribunals', *Herald*, 3 February 2020, <www.heraldscotland.com/news/18205603.concern-delay-smith-commissions-devolution-tribunals/?fbclid=IwAR3h76ScjdjJJZrl-2sP9CbjI7hH0_rUC36MFCIu-42JRSTuTi82mOnuUORI>.

Supreme Court. Judicial concerns have been voiced regarding the potential incompatibility of various aspects of the employment tribunal regime with human rights obligations imposed under the Human Rights Act 1998 (see, e.g., *PF Fort William* v *McLean* (2000), *The Times*, 11 August 2000 (failure to provide legal aid may be contrary to Article 6); and compare with *McVicar* v *UK* (2002) (failure to provide legal aid is not an automatic breach of Article 6: it is a question of fact and circumstances)).

## Employment Tribunal and EAT fees

In 2013 the Conservative Government under Prime Minister David Cameron, relying on the Tribunals, Courts and Enforcement Act 2007, enabled fees to be introduced for Employment and Employment Appeals Tribunals by way of SI 2013/1893. This Statutory Instrument allowed the Lord Chancellor to prescribe fees depending on the type of claim and the numbers of claimants involved.

If an individual brought a Type A claim the fee was £390, while for a Type B claim the fee was £1,200. Type A claims concerned relatively simple matters, such as complaints regarding time off for trade union activities and unauthorised deductions from wages. Type B claims were of the more complex variety and included cases of unfair dismissal and discrimination. If a claim was brought by a group of claimants', fees varied depending on the size of the group. Type A claims were:

- £780 for between two and ten people;
- £1,560 for between eleven and 200 people; and
- £2,340 for more than 200 people.

Type B claims were:

- £1,400 for between two and ten people;
- £4,800 for between eleven and 200 people; and
- £8,200 for more than 200 people.

Sundry other fees were also applicable for additional applications made during litigation. Unsurprisingly, such costs had an almost immediate impact on employment tribunal cases. In the year prior to fees having to be paid, 13,500 individual cases were, on average, heard per quarter. This dropped to 4,000 individual cases per quarter a year later.[3]

---

[3] House of Commons Briefing Paper Number 7081, 18 December 2017, 'Employment tribunal fees', Doug Pyper, Feargal McGuinness and Jennifer Brown.

However, following the landmark case *R (on the application of UNISON)* v *Lord Chancellor* brought by the trade union UNISON, in 2017 the Supreme Court ruled such fees illegal. The Supreme Court decided that the government had acted unlawfully and unconstitutionally in their introduction. Consequently, the fees were abolished and those who had paid them in the interim period were entitled to recompense, which in total was a not insubstantial sum of £32 million.

Figures released in May 2018 by the Ministry for Justice indicate that the number of employment law tribunal cases subsequently rose by 90 per cent between the last quarter of 2017 and the same period in 2016 when the fees were still in place.

## Legal aid funding and employment tribunals

Limited legal aid is available for complex employment tribunal cases in Scotland, but there is no legal aid funding for employment tribunals available in England and Wales. If an aggrieved employee is a member of a trade union, the trade union may pay for a solicitor. Some household insurers may also pay reasonable legal costs. It is important for potential litigants to check policy documents to see whether this cover applies to them.

If a claim is about discrimination, the Equality and Human Rights Commission may be able to provide some support. Unlike other courts, employment tribunals do not usually order either side to pay costs – or 'expenses' in Scotland – unless they decide that the litigant or employer acted unreasonably in bringing (or in the case of the employer, defending) the case, or if either or any of their representatives at the hearing behave unreasonably. In such instances, the employment tribunal can order one party to pay costs of up to £10,000. In exceptional circumstances, more can be awarded.

## Assistance by way of representation

'Assistance by way of representation' (ABWOR) is a specific type of funding available in certain circumstances under the Scottish Legal Aid system. Dependant on fulfilment of certain criteria, a party may qualify for help from a solicitor in preparing and representing them in their employment tribunal case.

In terms of Reg. 13(1) of the Advice and Assistance (Assistance by Way of Representation) (Scotland) Regulations 2003, the Scottish Legal Aid Board must give prior approval before a solicitor can provide ABWOR for proceedings before an employment tribunal.

## Ombudsmen

An 'ombudsman' (a concept imported from Scandinavia) is a public official whose function is to investigate complaints made by the public. Ombudsmen are present in both the public sector (handling complaints from members of the public who claim to have suffered 'injustice' against state bodies for misconduct ('maladministration')) and in the private sector (where complaints by consumers in relation to particular industries can be investigated).

### *Public bodies' maladministration*

The role of the ombudsman has changed radically in recent times where Scottish public bodies are involved. In the early post-devolution days, complaints of maladministration levied against public bodies in Scotland were made to the Scottish Parliamentary Commissioner for Administration (SPCA). The Scottish Public Services Ombudsman Act 2002, however, set up the new office of ombudsman to assume the role of the SPCA. The new Scottish Public Services Ombudsman (SPSO) also swallowed up the functions of other pre-existing officials including the Health Commissioner for Scotland, the Housing Association Ombudsman for Scotland and the Local Government Ombudsman. The SPSO is formally appointed by the monarch but, in practice, at the request of the Scottish Parliament.

The SPSO is the final stage for complaints about councils, the National Health Service, housing associations, colleges and universities, prisons, most water providers, the Scottish Government and its agencies and departments, and most Scottish authorities. The SPSO may hear complaints directly from members of the public and is empowered to launch investigations in this respect. In general, the SPSO is empowered to require any member or officer of the public body concerned to supply information or produce documents. The SPSO may also require the attendance of such persons for examination. Investigations may be followed by a report (or indeed a report may be written on a decision not to investigate).

### *Other ombudsmen*

Ombudsmen have also become a common feature of commercial life in Scotland. They can now be sought out by disaffected consumers in several industry sectors, including banking, insurance, estate agency, financial services and other business spheres. For example, the Financial Ombudsman Service helps sort out problems with banks, insurance, payment protection insurance, loans, mortgages and pensions, as well as with other money and financial complaints. The Property Ombudsman deals with complaints about estate agents, letting agents and other property professionals that are a member of its redress scheme, while the Energy Ombudsman can help with unresolved complaints about a gas or electricity company. The body that deals with complaints about lawyers in Scotland is the Scottish Legal Complaints Commission (more details of which can be found at: www.scottishlegalcomplaints.org.uk).

## Commissioners

The Scottish Parliament is statutorily responsible for nominating to Her Majesty, individuals for appointment to certain positions. These include the Scottish Information Commissioner, Scotland's Commissioner for Children and Young People and the Commissioner for Ethical Standards in Public Life in Scotland.

### Scottish Information Commissioner

The Scottish Information Commissioner's role is to promote the observance by public authorities of freedom of information legislation, by which 'a person who requests information from a Scottish public authority is entitled to be given it by the authority' by dint of s. 1(1) of the Freedom of Information (Scotland) Act 2002.

The Scottish Information Commissioner is chosen by a committee of MSPs set up for the purpose. Once selected, a motion to nominate the candidate is debated in the Scottish Parliament. The nomination is made by the Scottish Parliament to HM The Queen, who appoints the Scottish Information Commissioner. (Further details on the work of the Scottish Information Commissioner are available at: www.itspublicknowledge. info/home/ScottishInformationCommissioner.aspx)

### Scotland's Commissioner for Children and Young People

Scotland's Commissioner for Children and Young People promotes and safeguards the rights of children and young people. Created under the Commissioner for Children and Young People (Scotland) Act 2003, it is a position like that of Children's Ombudsman found in many other countries including Ireland, Norway and the United States.

The Commissioner for Children and Young People reviews law, policy and practice relating to the rights of children and young people with a view to assessing their adequacy and effectiveness. Specific regard must be had to any relevant provisions of the United Nations Convention on the Rights of the Child, especially those requiring that the best interests of the child be a primary consideration in decision making, and that due account be taken of the views of affected children and young people. The Commissioner cannot intervene in individual cases; however, these can highlight issues affecting a broader range of children and young people and this can be investigated by the Commissioner. After an investigation, the Commissioner can make recommendations to the Scottish Parliament on what action they feel is deemed appropriate. The Commissioner's duties apply to all children and young people under the age of eighteen, and all children and young people up to the age of twenty-one who have been in care or looked after by a local authority and are living in Scotland. The Commissioner is appointed on recommendation to HM The Queen following an interview by a committee of MSPs, and a committee of children and young people. (Further information about the role is available at: www.cypcs.org.uk)

### The Standards Commission for Scotland

The Ethical Standards in Public Life etc. (Scotland) Act 2000 provides a framework to encourage and, where necessary, enforce, high ethical standards in public life. The 2000 Act established the Standards Commission for Scotland and the post of Chief Investigating Officer, later renamed the 'Commissioner for Ethical Standards in Public Life' as amended by the Scottish Parliamentary Commissions and Commissioners etc. Act 2010. The 2010 Act also extended the oversight of the Standards Commission to include complaints about MSPs.

The Standards Commission for Scotland is an independent public body, responsible for encouraging high standards of behaviour by councillors and those appointed to boards of devolved public bodies. Its role is to encourage high ethical standards in public life, including the promotion and enforcement of the Codes of Conduct and to issue guidance to councils and devolved public bodies. It also adjudicates on alleged breaches of the Codes of Conduct, and where a breach is found, to apply a sanction.

### The Commissioner for Ethical Standards in Public Life

Complaints alleging breaches are investigated by the operationally independent Commissioner for Ethical Standards in Public Life in Scotland on behalf of the Standards Commission. The Commissioner is consequently responsible for investigating complaints about the conduct of MSPs, local authority councillors and members of public bodies, as well as regulating how people are appointed to the boards of public bodies in Scotland.

The post was established following the Ethical Standards in Public Life etc. (Scotland) Act 2000 as amended by the Scottish Parliamentary Commissions and Commissioners etc. Act 2010. The Commissioner for Ethical Standards in Public Life is appointed following interview by MSPs, debate in the Holyrood Parliament and then recommendation made to HM The Queen.

The Commissioner first decides whether the received complaint is relevant or if another body can assist the complainant, and must explain and convey its decision to the complainant. If an investigation is carried out, the Commissioner will produce a report for the Standards Commission. The Commission can then choose to direct the Commissioner to conduct further investigations, convene a hearing or do neither.

## ARBITRATION

Arbitration is a long-established mode of civil dispute resolution that has existed in some form in Scotland since the early thirteenth century (see Hunter (2002)). It also represents one of the rare areas of legal policy in Scotland where an Act of the Old Scottish Parliament, the 25th Article of Regulation 1695, has some import in the modern day.

Instead of resorting to civil litigation through the courts, in short, in an arbitration the disputing parties agree to appoint a private judge, termed an 'arbiter', to resolve their impasse. While reflecting the desire to avoid litigation, it is, however, important to note that arbitration is a binding, legally enforceable process. The arbiter's decision (or 'award') is usually final and the availability of appeals against decisions to the civil courts exists only in very limited circumstances.

Arbitration is, with some notable exceptions, a voluntary process in which parties choose to eschew litigation in its favour instead. Parties may simply agree to attempt arbitration when a dispute arises or may have previously entered a contract which binds them to attempt arbitration if any dispute pertaining to the contract occurs. In addition, the Advisory, Conciliation and Arbitration Service (ACAS) Arbitration Scheme (Great Britain) Order 2004 has empowered ACAS to prepare an arbitration scheme for the resolution of disputes arising from unfair dismissal claims.

### Arbitration conduct

Arbitration is a flexible process in Scotland, primarily regulated by common law principles established and refined by the courts over the centuries. Nevertheless, a number of statutory provisions do have a role to play, albeit largely on the fringes of arbitral practice, such as the 25th Article of

Regulation 1695, the Arbitration (Scotland) Act 1894 and the Administration of Justice (Scotland) Act 1972.

The common law basis of arbitration has resulted in a somewhat light regulatory touch, which allows the conduct of arbitral proceedings to be determined by the parties to the dispute. In terms of choice of arbiter, again the disputing parties may appoint any individual whomsoever. In practice, these are suitably qualified persons including solicitors or advocates of some professional standing and experience or, commonly, a professional imbued with relevant expertise and skill in the dispute area, such as an accountant, architect, surveyor or chartered engineer. In this sense, it can be argued that matters may be resolved more quickly and in a more informed fashion by those with appropriate technical skill and experience in the dispute area. Again, in practice, arbiters tend to be drawn from lists of accredited arbiters held by professional associations such as the Chartered Institute of Arbiters (Scotland) or the Academy of Experts. On occasion, disputing parties may be unable to reach agreement on appointment. Some commercial contracts, for example, will inherently make provision for both parties to appoint an arbiter. If two arbiters hearing a dispute cannot reach agreement on the award, provision may also be made for the appointment of a third arbiter, known as an 'oversman', to reach the final decision.

### Appeals in arbitration

As noted above, arbitration awards may be appealed in limited circumstances. Awards cannot be appealed on the facts. Historically, the main grounds of appeal include the following:

- 'Corruption', 'bribery' or 'falsehood' – these terms are found in the antiquated provisions of the aforementioned 25th Article of Regulation 1695. In practice, very few awards are overturned on this ground (*Morisons* v *Thomson's Trs* (1880)). Moreover, it has become clear that if an arbiter is negligent or makes an innocent error in making an award, it will not fall within these grounds for appeal (*Adams* v *Great North of Scotland Railway* (1891)).

- The arbiter must not have any undisclosed conflict of interest in the proceedings (*Sellar* v *Highland Railway* (1919)), although any such conflict of interest may be waived by the disputing parties (*Tancred, Arrol and Co.* v *Steel Co. of Scotland* (1890)).

- The award is defective or has gone beyond the terms of its reference (*ultra fines compromissi*) (an argument that was repelled by the court in *Karl Construction (Scotland) Limited* v *Sweeney Civil*

*Engineering (Scotland)* 2002)). Where an award is completely unintelligible or is in a form contrary to that which the parties specified then the court may reduce it. If the award is ambiguous but open to logical interpretation, then a court may place its own interpretation on it. The award must also exhaust the terms of the submission (*Donald* v *Shiell's Executrix* (1937)). By contrast, the award must pertain only to the issues put before the arbiter for his or her determination. Any other issues resolved by the arbiter may be ignored by the parties.

- Defective procedure – where the arbitral procedure does not conform to that prescribed by the parties or fails to be carried out in accordance with principles of natural justice, the award may be reduced on those grounds.

## Arbitration in practice

Arbitration procedures have become very popular in several different dispute areas. The principal attraction of arbitration is that it may be a quick, cost-effective, informal and confidential alternative to litigation through the civil courts. In practice, however, particularly in respect of commercial disputes, concerns have been raised that arbitration has in many senses become litigation by another name. The increased participation of lawyers in the arbitral process has generally led to commercial arbitration becoming an increasingly legalistic, formal and, therefore, expensive exercise. In addition, whereas in the civil courts the costs of court buildings and judges' salaries are met by the public purse, in arbitration, the costs of the arbiter, any legal clerk in attendance and the venue is met by the disputing parties.

To reverse some of the current deleterious trends in commercial arbitration in Scotland, and perceived deficiencies in its procedure, commentators have long called for the enactment of new arbitration laws (see Davidson (1993)). To this end, the Arbitration (Scotland) Act was introduced in 2010. The Act represents a significant shift from a primarily common law regime to one based primarily upon statutory provisions. The founding principles of the Arbitration (Scotland) Act 2010 are that the object of arbitration is to resolve disputes fairly, impartially and without unnecessary delay or expense. Parties should be free to agree how to resolve disputes subject only to such safeguards as are necessary in the public interest and that the court should not intervene in arbitration except as provided for in the Act. (Further details may be found at: www. legislation.gov.uk/asp/2010/1/contents)

## Adjudication in construction disputes

Under the Housing Grants, Construction and Regeneration Act 1996, the use of adjudication is compelled in most construction contracts to resolve disputes arising therefrom. This short form of arbitration involving determination of disputes by a designated expert is thus imposed upon the parties. Moreover, any awards issued have 'temporary finality' (i.e., they are rendered binding until the contract is completed). Enthusiasts have pointed to its main benefit in representing an inexpensive, speedy process that allows for the expediting of construction contracts. Contrarily, it could be argued that such adjudication in practice leads to poorly informed decisions. Moreover, the fact that due to its temporary finality, awards stemming from this new procedure can be challenged after completion of the contract, which may mean that in practice adjudication commonly represents merely an additional step in the process of dispute resolution. It should also be noted that the compulsory nature of the procedure and tight time frames for dispute determination may entail certain human rights concerns (see Macauley (2000)).

## ALTERNATIVE DISPUTE RESOLUTION

Modern times have seen the seeking out and development of new, generally more consensual, alternative dispute resolution (ADR). The dominant ADR procedure is known as 'mediation'. In mediation the parties are encouraged to reach their own solution to their impasse by means of a third-party neutral or 'mediator'. As well as being a consensual process, the ethos behind mediation is party empowerment, which is unlike traditional litigation and arbitration where decisions are imposed upon the litigants by someone else. Other perceived benefits to mediation include its speed and low costs compared to traditional means of resolving disputes.

Although the resolution of employment disputes using consensual methods by ACAS can be seen as the forerunner in Scotland as regards ADR, developments in ADR have since also taken place in the family, commercial and neighbourhood disputes arenas, as well as in criminal matters. Outwith family and community matters, mediation practice in Scotland has historically remained modest, albeit that some progress seems to have been made in more recent times. Barriers to mediation's development may include a lack of recognised standards in the regulation and training of neutrals, ignorance of, and perhaps active resistance to, mediation on the part of both lawyers and disputing parties, and the fact that mediation can never guarantee settlement. (Clark, *Lawyers and Mediation*, 2012).

**Mediation in family disputes**

The first family mediation developments took place in Scotland in the late 1980s when a pilot programme was established in the Lothian region. Since then family mediation has developed across Scotland under an umbrella organisation, 'Relationships Scotland', and a group of family lawyer specialists termed 'Comprehensive Accredited Lawyer Mediators' (or CALM). Mediation services may be offered in respect of disputes pertaining to the custody of, and access to, children and financial and property settlements arising from legal separation or divorce. In matrimonial matters, both the Sheriff Courts and the Court of Session have been empowered since 1994 to refer disputing parties to mediation if it is deemed appropriate (Ordinary Cause Rules, r. 33.22; Rules of the Court of Session 1994, r. 49.23).

**Commercial mediation**

Several private, for-profit, commercial mediation providers also now operate in Scotland, including 'Core Mediation' and 'Catalyst Mediation'. Commercial mediation has not developed as quickly in Scotland as was hitherto expected; however, the introduction of the high-profile, in-court advice and mediation project in Edinburgh Sheriff Court in the early 2000s may have served to increase publicity in and for this relatively new form of dispute resolution (see Samuel (2002)).

In 2001 under the Act of Sederunt (Ordinary Cause Rules) Amendment (Commercial Actions), Sheriff Court rules were amended and sheriffs could refer parties to mediation in appropriate cases. Under Rule 40.12(3)(m), a sheriff has since also had the power to make any order that he or she thinks will result in the speedy resolution of the action – including the use of ADR.

**Simple procedure and ADR**

The introduction of 'simple procedure' has encouraged the increased use of mediation and negotiation. This was enhanced recently by the Act of Sederunt (Simple Procedure) 2016 SSI 2016/200 Schedule 1 that introduced new Sheriff Court Simple Procedure Rules.

Simple procedure is a court process designed to provide a speedy, inexpensive and informal way to resolve disputes where the monetary value in dispute does not exceed £5,000. Under SSI 2016/200 1.2(4), the fourth of its five principles of sheriff court procedure states that: 'parties are to be encouraged to settle their disputes by negotiation or alternative dispute resolution, and should be able to do so throughout the progress of a case.' It adds, under 'Sheriffs Powers' at 1.8 (2), that: 'the sheriff may do anything or give any order considered necessary to encourage negotiation or alternative dispute resolution between the parties.'

There is still, however, no formal recognition by the civil justice system in Scotland of mediation *per se* to settle disputes. This is slowly changing and began because of views expressed in the review of access to civil justice in Scotland by Lord Gill, and subsequent support given to it by the Scottish Government. His Scottish Civil Courts Review of September 2009 included a chapter on the use of mediation. Here, Gill recommended that litigation should remain at the forefront of dispute resolution, and that mediation is applicable only to certain types of case and should be used cautiously. This did not discourage the Scottish Government to comment in response:

> Overall, though, we believe Lord Gill is right in his diagnosis and right in his prescription. It is now for the Scottish Government, the judiciary and the Scottish Court Service to ensure that this landmark report leads to the fair, just, accessible and efficient civil justice system that Scotland deserves. (Kenny MacAskill MSP, Minister for Justice, November 2010, 'Scottish Government Response to the Report and Recommendations of the Scottish Civil Courts Review Ministerial Foreword 2009'.)

Further impetus to a more structured, formal and expansive use of mediation is seen in the recommendations coming from the 'Report to the Cabinet Secretary for Health and Sport into Cultural Issues Related to Allegations of Bullying and Harassment in NHS Highland', published in April 2019 by John Sturrock QC. Here Sturrock called for the creation of the Early Dispute Resolution Office. Its function would be to review all public-sector cases received by the relevant court or tribunal, identify and direct appropriate cases towards mediation (or other more appropriate forms of dispute resolution) and to coordinate the mediation process. The Report leaves open the extent to which mediation should be made mandatory and suggests possible opt outs that the Report terms 'special cause exemptions'.

## Mediation in community/neighbourhood disputes

Mediation programmes have become a feature of community life in Scotland in recent years. Several schemes in Edinburgh, Dundee, Kirkcaldy, Livingston and Glenrothes have been established since 1995 under the aegis of charitable bodies such as UK Mediation and Safer

Communities Reducing Offending (SACRO). Such programmes, operated by locally trained volunteer mediators, seek to assist members of the community to resolve a wide range of typical neighbourhood disputes, including noise pollution, problems with the behaviour of children and pets, harassment and boundary issues. (For a review of some of the early Scottish schemes, see Mackay and Brown (1998).)

## Scottish Mediation

The organisation Scottish Mediation was established in 1990 to raise the profile of mediation in Scotland, as well as to act as a professional body for mediators in Scotland, maintain the Scottish Mediation Register of practitioners and provide access to quality assured mediation services. By so doing, it seeks to:

- promote a wider understanding of the appropriate use of mediation in conflict management and prevention;
- support and promote education, training and research in skills and best practice;
- create and encourage links between mediators and the Scottish public, private, voluntary and community organisations; and
- promote and organise standards of professional conduct and training.

### Bringing mediation into the mainstream in civil justice in Scotland

As suggested above, a more formalised use of mediation in the civil justice process in Scotland is gradually gaining support. This has been helped by a number of significant mediation developments, including:

- more encouragement of ADR by the courts since the introduction in 2016 of simple procedure;
- a report of the Justice Committee of the Scottish Parliament in 2018; and
- a consultation for a proposed Member's Bill on mediation in Scotland in May 2019.

Consultation for the Member's Bill closed in August 2019 and cross-party support was subsequently sought and gained from fifty-four supporting MSPs. As a result, the Bill's proposer Margaret Mitchell MSP earned the right to formally introduce it up until 1 June 2020. However, the coronavirus emergency throughout 2020 frustrated the normal business of the Scottish Parliament and her Bill went no further. It may well return in the future as mediation has now captured the attention of both the Scottish Parliament and Government.

Of some significance to its possible success is Scottish Mediation's report 'Bringing Mediation into the Mainstream in Civil Justice in Scotland' (June 2019). The report was the culmination of work done by an Expert Group put together by Scottish Mediation that consisted of representatives of the judiciary, advocates, solicitors, the third sector, mediation services, consumer interest and the small-business community, as well as Scottish Mediation itself and the Scottish Government. Its remit was to investigate how a greater use of mediation could be encouraged in Scotland's civil justice system. It made twenty-seven recommendations, with their thrust captured in its desire to 'normalise' the use of mediation in the civil justice system as a 'viable option in addition to, and often instead of, litigation', including introducing a mandatory requirement on disputing parties to attend a session about mediation, by way of a Scottish Mediation Act.

'Bringing Mediation into the Mainstream in Civil Justice in Scotland' prompted a positive reaction from the Scottish Government, as contained in 'The Scottish Government Response to the Independent Review of Mediation in Scotland' (December 2019). It states that 'it is clear that mediation should have a bigger role to play in helping citizens resolve disputes'. Although with an eye to Gill and others, the Scottish Government also notes that the right to access the court process by disputants should always be preserved. The Scottish Government considers that a series of questions arise out of the Report that must be resolved before legislation is introduced. To this end, during 2020 they intend a public consultation on mediation and wider dispute resolution reforms. They also wish to collaborate with key stakeholders in establishing a 'Collaborative Partnership on Dispute Resolution' and a 'Scottish Dispute Resolution Delivery Group' to progress new policy in the area. It further indicates that it would give careful consideration to legislation on mediation 'if and when it is formally introduced to Parliament'. A caveat being that systematic reform is needed in a number of areas and that any legislation would require tackling these simultaneously to bring mediation into the mainstream to avoid limited effect.

## DIVERSIONS FROM PROSECUTION

The Community Justice (Scotland) Act 2016 has seen the consolidation of a range of initiatives where offending behaviour is dealt with in an alternative manner rather than through the normal criminal court process. The aim of such 'diversion from prosecution' is two-fold: first, to introduce alternatives into the criminal justice system when dealing with perpetrators of minor crime; and, second, a belief that handling certain types of offence in a different way may lead to superior outcomes – particularly in pursuance of the aim of reducing recidivism (re-offending) and, in some cases, meeting the needs of victims more effectively. While some might claim that these kinds of initiative are soft options, pandering to liberal ideologies, many programmes have in practice been successful in meeting at least some of these objectives.

## Fiscal fines

The Criminal Justice (Scotland) Act 1987 made provision for a 'fiscal fine', where, in respect of the commission of minor crimes or summary offences, an accused person would simply be fined instead of being prosecuted through the court. The powers in this regard have since been extended by the Criminal Justice (Scotland) Act 1995.

In general, if the accused person accepts an offer by the procurator fiscal to pay a fiscal fine then the prosecution does not proceed, and the accused receives no criminal record. Under s. 50 of the Criminal Proceedings etc. (Reform) (Scotland) Act 2007, fiscal fines can vary between £50 and £300; however, a compensation offer may be issued either separately or additionally with similar effect but with payment going to the victim of the crime rather than the state – these can be of any amount not exceeding £5,000.

## Diversion to a voluntary organisation

This kind of diversion from prosecution may occur where there is deemed to be no public interest in prosecuting an individual. Instead, the offender may be offered an opportunity to attend an appropriate voluntary organisation, which may, for example, deal with any drug or alcohol dependency that has fuelled the commission of their crime.

## Restorative justice

Several pilot schemes utilising mediation as a diversion from prosecution have been developed throughout Scotland by SACRO. These refer accused persons to mediation programmes where they attend face-to-face sessions with the victims of their crimes and provide some form of compensation to their victims instead of being prosecuted through the criminal courts. It is argued that such programmes may benefit offenders in helping them to see the error of their ways (and hence reduce re-offending), and also be of value to victims, whose psychological and material needs may be addressed more effectively than through the court system.

## Fixed penalty notices

Fixed penalties are commonplace in respect of minor road-traffic offences such as speeding, driving without insurance or failing to wear a seat-belt. Payment of a set amount will result in no prosecution being brought against the driver. Many such offences also result, of course, in the endorsement of the perpetrator's driving licence.

## Problem solving: drug courts

Drug courts were piloted in Glasgow and Fife in 2001 and 2002. The Fife Drug Court was closed in 2013 due to insufficient court capacity. The aim of these special courts was and is to divert offenders, whose criminal behaviour has been fuelled by drug dependency, from an oft-continuous replay of prosecution through the courts, into medical treatment pro-grammes. The intention is that appropriate medical treatment may deal with the root cause of the offending behaviour and thus lead to the reha-bilitation of the individual concerned.

Whether drug courts have been a success is debatable. In a report of November 2009, it was stated that 70 per cent of those individuals han-dled by the drug courts were re-convicted within a year and 82 per cent within two years (see 'Review of the Glasgow and Fife Drug Courts Report', Community Justice Services Scottish Government (2009)).

## Problem solving: alcohol courts

In a similar vein, problem-solving alcohol courts have recently become a feature of Scotland's legal landscape. And as with the drug courts, they have a philosophy of diversion about them, particularly regarding future recidivism.

An Alcohol Problem Court was introduced as a pilot scheme at Edin-burgh Sheriff Court in 2016. Considered a success, similar pilot schemes have since been extended to Aberdeen and Forfar; and from Spring 2018 also to Glasgow. From the outset such courts apply to an accused who lives locally, particularly those aged under thirty-five, appearing in the Sheriff Summary Courts who, with similar previous convictions, pleads guilty to, or is convicted of, charges involving violence (except domestic violence), dishonesty, public order offences or drink-driving offences in circumstances in which it appears or is accepted that alcohol abuse has significantly contributed to their offending. If the presiding sheriff at the time of plea or conviction forms the view that an offender falling within those parameters may benefit from the problem-solving approach that the court will adopt, the sheriff will request an Alcohol

Court Assessment Report and defer sentence to the next suitable alcohol court.

The aim of the pilots is to deliver sentences which are tailored to influence an individual's behaviour and hold them accountable, with progress expected to be rigorously monitored by the same sheriff. The pilot scheme in Glasgow is supported by Glasgow City Health and Social Care Partnership. Similar support is found in Edinburgh, Aberdeen and Forfar.

## Fatal accident inquiries

After the occurrence of a fatal accident in Scotland (e.g., in the workplace), a fatal accident inquiry will be held. The equivalent in England is a coroner's inquest. The purpose of a fatal accident inquiry is to ascertain the facts surrounding the death rather than to apportion any blame, as such. The inquiry is set up by the Procurator Fiscal and takes place in the Sheriff Court. During the inquiry, evidence will be led, and submissions made in court by the procurator fiscal.

Any interested parties such as relatives, employers or colleagues may be called upon to take part in the inquiry and may be represented at the inquiry by lawyers. At the conclusion of evidence and submissions, the sheriff will make a determination setting out the circumstances of the death, indicating where and when the accident resulting in the death took place, along with the causes of both the accident and the death itself.

---

### Essential Facts

- Tribunals are provided by the state as a means by which administrative, employment, land and other forms of dispute can be resolved without proceedings in the civil courts. Tribunals are perceived to be characterised by the benefits of flexibility, speed, informality and openness.
- Arbitration involves the resolution of disputes by a private judge known as an 'arbiter'. Arbitration is common in commercial matters and represents a legally enforceable process in which appeals of arbitral awards are available only in very limited circumstances.
- Ombudsmen are officials who can investigate complaints made by the public in several areas found in both the public and private sector.

- The ADR process known as mediation sees disputants being assisted by a mediator to help resolve their dispute. Perceived benefits of mediation include speed, affordability, informality, party empowerment and confidentiality. Mediation is common in family matters but not so much in other civil dispute areas; although this trend is slowly changing and may soon be formalised into the legal landscape in Scotland.
- Children's hearing panels are a well-established method in Scotland for dealing with children under the age of sixteen in need of compulsory care orders.
- There are several alternatives in Scotland that seek to divert offenders from prosecution in the criminal courts. These include fiscal fines, drug and alcohol courts and criminal mediation programmes.

## Essential Cases

*S* v *Miller* (2001): legal aid being unavailable for children's hearings might be inconsistent with a child's right to a fair trial under Article 6 of the ECHR; reforms have been enacted to provide for legal aid in some circumstances.

*Morisons* v *Thomson's Trs* (1880): it is not corrupt for an arbiter to first request a loan of £1,000 from one party in a dispute that he was arbitrating and then request the same from the other party; the arbiter knew both parties, so any undue influence was unlikely to arise in the circumstances.

*Donald* v *Shiell's Executrix* (1937): an arbitration sought determination of two issues in dispute regarding the rights of incoming and outgoing farm tenants; it failed to deal with both issues, so entire terms of award could be reduced.

## Website resources

### Access to justice
The Scottish Government

www.gov.scot/policies/access-to-justice/tribunals-system/

### About Scottish tribunals
SCT

https://www.scotcourts.gov.uk/the-courts/the-tribunals/about-scottish-tribunals

Copy and paste into your browser

### Fifty most recent Upper Tribunal decisions in Scotland
SCT

www.scotcourts.gov.uk/search-judgments/upper-tribunal-decisions

### Ombudsman and Commissioners in Scotland
CAB

https://www.citizensadvice.org.uk/scotland/law-and-courts/civil-rights/complaints1/how-to-use-an-ombudsman-or-commissioner-in-scotland-s/

Copy and paste into your browser

### Alternative dispute resolution guide
Unlock the Law

www.unlockthelaw.co.uk/alternative-dispute-resolution-guide.html

### Children's hearings
The Scottish Government

www.gov.scot/policies/child-protection/childrens-hearings/

### Children's hearings: the essential legal guide
Unlock the Law

www.unlockthelaw.co.uk/childrens-hearings-scotland.html

### Alternatives to prosecution
COPFS

www.copfs.gov.uk/about-us/what-we-do/10-about-us/297-alternative-to-prosecution

## Video resources

**SCTS corporate induction film**

Scottish Courts and Tribunals Service

https://youtu.be/llkK-uDc_h8

**Children and Young Peoples Commissioner Scotland**

Our commitments to children: How are Scotland and the UK doing?

https://www.facebook.com/CYPCS/videos/our-commitments-to-children-how-are-scotland-and-the-uk-doing/481386302470281/

**Family mediation individual session**

CALM

https://youtu.be/y6MU0OkzyWs

**What happens at mediation?**

CALM

https://youtu.be/oV8EYQwo-KU

**What is a children's hearing?**

The Children's Reporter

https://youtu.be/0pTfoOgOJ1E

**An Introduction to children's hearings**

Moray Council

https://youtu.be/74HZBKyjoEc

# 5   LEGAL PERSONNEL

In this chapter we review some of the key actors in the Scottish legal system, including legal professionals, legal officials of the Crown, judges and jurors.

## SOLICITORS

The Scottish legal profession can be broken into two distinct streams of lawyer: solicitors and advocates. By far the most prevalent is the solicitor. The Law Society of Scotland (LSS) tells us that there are around 11,000 practising solicitors in Scotland at present.

Solicitors' work may vary significantly. The wide range includes giving legal advice to the public, drawing up legal documents, organising the affairs and distributing the estates of deceased persons, undertaking the buying and selling of land and buildings (known as 'conveyancing') and court work. Solicitors can thus properly be viewed as 'general practitioners' of the law. Solicitors may hold many different employment arrangements, including working in private practice, either alone, in partnership or working as employees for such law firms; working 'in-house' for large commercial concerns; or as employees of public and local authorities.

### Legal Services (Scotland) Act 2010

The controversial Legal Services (Scotland) Bill was passed by the Scottish Parliament on 6 October 2010 and was given Royal Assent on 9 November 2010. The aim of the Legal Services (Scotland) Act 2010 is to remove restrictions contained in the Solicitors (Scotland) Act 1980 regarding how solicitors can organise their businesses. The Legal Services (Scotland) Act 2010 now allows solicitors to form partnerships with non-solicitors in what are termed 'alternative business structures'. Known colloquially as 'Tesco Law', the Act enables investment from outside the profession from supermarkets, banks or accountants, among others, although a 51 per cent majority share in any such business must remain with solicitors or other regulated professionals.

### Rights of audience

As noted above, some solicitors represent their clients in both the criminal and civil courts. Historically speaking, solicitors did not enjoy 'rights of audience' – that is, the right to appear on behalf of clients in the superior courts (e.g., the Court of Session, the High Court of Justiciary and the House of Lords (now the Supreme Court). By virtue of the provisions of the Solicitors (Scotland) (Rights of Audience in the Court of Session, the House of Lords and the Judicial Committee of the Privy Council) Rules 2002, solicitors may now undertake further training and qualify as a 'solicitor-advocate'. Designation as a solicitor-advocate grants the individual extended rights of audience to appear in Scotland's superior courts.

Non-lawyers (other than the parties themselves) have no rights of audience in the Scottish courts. Some notable exceptions to this rule include the simple procedure for small claims in the Sheriff Court and certain sheriff court proceedings under the Debtors (Scotland) Act 1987, where suitable non-lawyers may be given permission by the court to represent parties.

## Regulation

The Legal Services (Scotland) Act 2010 also introduced a new Regulatory Committee independent from the Council of the Law Society of Scotland, which from 1949 had previously overseen solicitors in Scotland. Consisting of five non-solicitor and five solicitor members, its remit sees all regulatory sub-committees of the LSS reporting directly to it rather than the Society's Council. Every practising solicitor must be a member of the LSS and may only practise law if issued with an LSS 'practising certificate'.

The LSS has several functions, principally including responsibility for setting appropriate admission, education and ongoing professional development standards; standards of practice; and disciplining misconduct.

## Scottish Solicitors' Discipline Tribunal

In serious cases of misconduct, solicitors may be cited to appear before a Scottish Solicitors' Discipline Tribunal established under the Solicitors (Scotland) Act 1980, as amended. The tribunal is empowered to issue a fine of up to £10,000, suspend or disbar the solicitor from practice, in addition to ordering the retraining of any staff involved in the complaint.

## Scottish Legal Complaints Commission

The LSS also promotes the interests of its members and acts as a pressure group in the political system. The extent to which these two functions can co-exist in the same body has been questioned. In response to such concerns, as of 1 October 2008, complaints regarding the *service* provided by legal practitioners (both solicitors and advocates) have been dealt with by the new, independent Scottish Legal Complaints Commission. As noted above, complaints regarding alleged professional *misconduct* of solicitors are still dealt with by the LSS, and complaints in respect of advocates by the Faculty of Advocates.

## Guarantee fund

The LSS is responsible for the maintenance of a 'guarantee fund', to which all solicitors must contribute. The fund is used to meet the compensation needs of clients who have suffered financial loss at the hands of errant solicitors. In this sense, solicitors may be held personally liable in damages for their negligent acts through civil court actions brought by disaffected clients. Solicitors are thus under a general delictual duty to act with due diligence and skill and hence must act in such a fashion as might reasonably be expected of skilled, legal professionals (for some examples, see *Evans* v *Stool* (1885); and *Stewart* v *McLean, Baird and Neilson* (1915)).

## Training

Most solicitors will have first gained a law degree (LLB) from a Scottish university, followed by the more vocationally oriented university taught diploma in legal practice (DipLP), known from September 2011 as PEAT 1 (Professional Education and Training Part 1). After PEAT 1, the fledgling solicitor undertakes a two-year 'traineeship' within private practice or with a public authority, and attends a two-week professional competence course prior to receiving their practising certificate. This work-based element is called PEAT 2.

Due to fewer trainee vacancies than in previous times, and in a bid to attract a more diverse workforce, there is a more flexible approach to PEAT 1 and 2 training today that allows budding solicitors to complete these essential elements on a part-time basis if necessary, although naturally over a longer period.

All solicitors, much like many other professions, are under a continuing obligation to bolster and update their professional skills by annually undertaking several hours of continuing professional development (or CPD).

## Notaries public

Many solicitors are also notaries public. This is an old professional role which, since 1896, can be assumed only by solicitors. The functions of a notary public include attesting or authenticating powers of attorney, particularly abroad; the administration of oaths; and activities in respect of certain commercial and maritime documents.

## ADVOCATES

Advocates are far less common in number than solicitors, with around 500 currently in practice. At least traditionally, advocates can be said to represent the elite of the legal profession in Scotland, although some solicitors (and other commentators) might argue with that! As a reflection of this view, advocates have historically held exclusive rights of audience in the superior Scottish courts. This monopoly, however, was removed with the introduction of solicitor-advocates in 2002, who also now enjoy rights of representation in such courts.

Advocates can be further split into 'junior counsel' and 'senior counsel', also termed 'Queen's Counsel' (QC). An advocate may be appointed to the status of QC after gaining appropriate experience and reputation. This process is known as 'taking silk', so named as the advocate is entitled, on becoming a QC, to wear a silk robe in court rather than a woollen one. The profession of advocate is known collectively as 'the Bar', a term derived from the bar that runs along one side of the Court of Session, behind which advocates stand in court.

Advocates are sole practitioners and, unlike solicitors, are barred by their professional rules from establishing partnerships (although they may work together on a case). Advocates are attached to 'stables', being groupings of advocates. Each stable is serviced by a clerk who takes instructions from solicitors and distributes work to their stable advocates. Examples of stables are Ampersand, Arnot Manderson Advocates, Axiom Advocates and Black Chambers, among others. A separate service company, Faculty Services Ltd, provides administrative and secretarial support.

A quirk of the system that may perplex readers is that the client is generally not able to contract or make any contact with an advocate directly, but may only do so through the offices of a solicitor. It also generally follows that in respect of meetings between an advocate and his or her client, a solicitor must be present. Having said that, persons belonging to professional bodies (e.g., architects, surveyors and engineers) may instruct advocates directly.

'Opinions of counsel' are often sought from advocates. In this sense we are referring to advice sought by a party through their solicitor about, for example, interpretation of an area of law or the analysis of some contractual provision where an element of doubt exists. The advocate's opinion may often be sought by parties contemplating involvement in litigation proceedings. The advice may give such parties a more informed view of their legal position and indicate their prospects of success.

## Regulation

Under the Legal Services (Scotland) Act 2010, the Court of Session is responsible for admitting persons to the public office of advocate and for laying down criteria and procedure for admission. The Court of Session has delegated responsibility for prescribing the criteria and procedure for admission to the Faculty of Advocates.

Scottish advocates are regulated by the Faculty of Advocates. This body is headed by the Dean of the Faculty and, like the Law Society of Scotland, its principal remit is to set appropriate standards for admission, qualifications and professional conduct. Any rules that the Faculty makes in this regard are subject to approval by the Lord President of the Court of Session. Service complaints made against advocates (as with solicitors) are dealt with by the Scottish Legal Complaints Commission. Although most disciplinary cases regarding professional misconduct are handled in-house through a 'complaints committee', more serious cases may be remitted to a 'discipline tribunal', which is empowered to censure, issue a fine of up to £15,000, suspend or disbar an advocate from practice.

In what may seem to be a somewhat inequitable proposition, unlike the case with solicitors, it is a customary rule of law that advocates cannot be sued in the civil courts for negligence; albeit that a remedy may arise where an advocate had acted fraudulently (see, e.g., *Swinfen v Lord Chelmsford* (1860)).

## Training

The route to becoming an advocate, at least initially, mirrors that for solicitors. Most advocates hold a university law degree and diploma in legal practice. This legal education is generally followed by a year's work as an 'intrant' trainee in a legal office, followed by engagement for a nine-month period as a pupil of an established advocate, a process known as 'devilling'. Perhaps redolent of the traditionally elitist nature of the advocacy profession, devilling is normally carried out for no payment, although scholarships are now available.

## CONVEYANCING AND EXECUTRY PRACTITIONERS AND PARALEGALS

In a move that took away a what had been a monopoly for solicitors, two new forms of legal professional – licensed conveyancers and executry practitioners – were established by the Law Reform (Miscellaneous Provisions) (Scotland) Act 1990. A Scottish Conveyancing and Executry

Services Board was set up to regulate these new occupational roles. The provisions of the 1990 Act created something of a hullabaloo, particularly as it was felt by solicitors that the conveyancing market would become saturated and fees would drop to rock-bottom levels (colloquially termed 'bucket conveyancing'). Such fears have proved largely unfounded, however, primarily because these new vocational opportunities have not proven particularly popular. The Conveyancing and Executry Services Board was abolished in 2003 by way of the Public Bodies and Public Appointments etc. (Scotland) Act 2003. The Board's functions have now been transferred to the Conveyancing and Executry Practitioners Committee of the Law Society of Scotland.

Other types of often part-qualified legal professional, who are broadly termed 'paralegals', frequently work in support of solicitors in many different legal spheres, particularly doing conveyancing, executries and criminal work.

## LAW OFFICERS OF THE CROWN

The Law Officers of the Crown are the Crown's official legal advisers. The two principal officers – the Lord Advocate and the Solicitor General for Scotland – are political appointments and members of the Scottish Government. They represent the Crown in Scotland in both criminal and civil matters. In addition, the Lord Advocate is the head of the Crown Office and thus has ultimate responsibility for overseeing criminal prosecutions in Scotland. Advocates Depute, appointed by the Lord Advocate, appear in the bulk of High Court of Justiciary cases. On rare occasions, either the Lord Advocate or the Solicitor General will themselves appear.

Procurators fiscal, and deputes, represent the Crown in cases in the inferior criminal courts. By virtue of the Scotland Act 1998, the Lord Advocate and the Solicitor General are appointed by the Queen, but in practice appointment is made on the recommendation of the First Minister and with the approval of the Scottish Parliament.

A third Scottish Crown Law Officer – the Advocate General for Scotland – is a member of the UK Government. The role of the Advocate General is to offer advice to the Westminster Government on legal issues pertaining to Scotland.

## THE JUDICIARY

In common with England and Wales, there is no separate professional grouping that constitutes the judiciary. The relevant qualifications for the judiciary are outlined in the discussion of the courts in Chapter 3. The judiciary comprises suitably experienced and skilled members of either the solicitors' or, more commonly, the advocates' profession.

The fact that there exists no separate profession of judges, akin, for example, to that which exists in the French legal system, can be criticised on the basis that the role of judge is fundamentally different from the role of solicitor or advocate. Nevertheless, any newly appointed members of the judiciary would have gained significant experience of the court process and necessarily the analytical legal skills developed as lawyers, both clearly relevant to the judicial role.

Another important policy issue regarding the judiciary pertains to the wide and varied nature of legal issues in the docket of cases that judges may be required to determine. These often span the whole gamut of civil and criminal law. This wide range may raise doubts as to the ability of our custodians of justice to apply the law in a correct fashion in every case that comes before them. In terms of different legal spheres, the judiciary may have to be 'jacks of all trades', although many may be legitimately described as 'masters of most'.

## Appointments

Scotland's most senior judges – the Lord President and the Lord Justice Clerk – are technically appointed by the Crown on the advice of the Prime Minister, who himself or herself receives recommendations from the First Minister following advice of an independent selection panel who has interviewed, selected and advised on the most suitable candidate.

## Judicial Appointments Board

Before 2001, Court of Session and High Court judges and sheriffs were appointed to office by the Crown acting on the recommendation of the Secretary of State for Scotland. The Lord Advocate also played an advisory role in such judicial appointments. In light of concerns voiced regarding a lack of transparency and accountability in the incumbent system (including disquiet about the fact that the Lord Advocate may recommend his or her own elevation to the Bench), and potential incompatibilities with human rights obligations, a Judicial Appointments Board comprising senior judges and lay members was set up in 2001 by the Justice Minister to oversee the recruitment and appointment of judges.

The legislation now governing the operation of the Judicial Appointments Board for Scotland is found in the Judiciary and Courts (Scotland) Act 2008 that came into force with the Judiciary and Courts (Scotland)

Act 2008 (Commencement No. 2) Order 2009. The Board is an advisory body whose remit is to make recommendations to Scottish Ministers on the appointment to the offices of Judge of the Court of Session, the Chair of the Scottish Land Court, sheriffs principal, sheriffs and part-time sheriffs.

## Scottish courts and tribunals services

The Scottish Judiciary are holders of specific judicial offices set out in the Judiciary and Courts (Scotland) Act 2008. On 1 April 2010, the Act also established the Scottish Court Service as an independent statutory body. Previously, the organisation was an Executive Agency of the Scottish Government accountable to Scottish Ministers. Now called the Scottish Courts and Tribunals Services under the Courts Reform (Scotland) Act 2014, the Scottish Courts and Tribunals Services has assumed the responsibilities of both the former Scottish Court Service and the Scottish Tribunals Service.

## Judges

The Act also appointed the Lord President as head of the Scottish judiciary. In this role, the Lord President has responsibility for:

- the efficient disposal of business throughout the courts;
- the welfare, guidance and training of the judiciary; and
- ensuring appropriate arrangements are in place for the investigation and determination of complaints about judicial conduct.

In these functions the Lord President is supported by the Judicial Office for Scotland, which is a separate part of the Scottish Courts and Tribunals Service.

The office of Lord President is the most senior judicial office in Scotland and the office holder is responsible for leadership of the entire Scottish judiciary, in addition to chairing the Board of the Scottish Court Service. The role of the Judicial Appointments Board is to interview applicants through an open selection process and pass on its recommendations to the First Minister. It should also be noted that on implementation of the Constitutional Reform Act 2005 in October 2009, an independent selection commission comprising, *inter alia*, a member of the Scottish Judicial Appointments Board and a member from its counterparts in England and Wales, and Northern Ireland now appoint members to the new Supreme Court.

Generally, judges appointed prior to 31 March 1995 must retire before the age of seventy-five. Those appointed thereafter are bound to retire at the age of seventy (subject to an eligibility to sit as 'retired judges' until the age of seventy-five).

## Sheriffs

Sheriffs are again appointed by the Crown, on the recommendation of the First Minister as advised by the Judicial Appointments Board for Scotland. The Judicial Appointments Board considers applications from those seeking appointment and furnishes recommendations in this sense to the First Minister. Sheriffs appointed prior to 31 March 1995 must retire at the age of seventy-two. Those appointed thereafter are bound to retire at seventy years old. Part-time sheriffs – up to a maximum of eighty – may be appointed by the First Minister from time to time, as the need arises.

Until recently stipendiary magistrates were also appointed by the First Minister on the recommendation of a Stipendiary Magistrates Advisory Committee constituted by the relevant sheriff principal. However, the office of stipendiary magistrate was abolished following the passage of the Courts Reform (Scotland) Act 2014 and replaced with the new office of summary sheriff.

## Summary sheriff

The post of summary sheriff was created to ensure that cases in Scotland's courts are heard at the appropriate level in the court structure, enabling sheriffs to focus on solemn business and more complex criminal cases. Summary sheriffs sit in the Sheriff Courts and their criminal jurisdiction is in respect of summary prosecutions. They also have competence in civil proceedings concerning domestic abuse; adoption; children's hearings; forced marriage; warrants and interim orders; diligence proceedings; extension of time to pay debts and simple procedure. The procedure for appointment of summary sheriffs is the same as that for sheriffs.

## Justice of the peace

A justice of the peace (JP) is a layperson who hears criminal cases in the local courts, such as those regarding theft, assault, breach of the peace and road traffic offences. In general, they are not legally qualified. A legally qualified person can become a JP but cannot act in any proceedings in a Justice of the Peace Court within their own sheriffdom.

Justices of the peace are appointed on the recommendation of Justice of the Peace Advisory Committees (or JPACs) under procedures approved by the Scottish Government and make a vital contribution to the community. Under the Criminal Proceedings etc. (Reform) (Scotland) Act 2007, such

JP appointees serve in Scotland's Justice of the Peace Courts. Justice of the Peace Courts are managed by the Scottish Courts and Tribunals Service. Since 2007, such courts have been involved in increasingly more serious cases, where their powers are considered appropriate. Their judgments can be appealed to the High Court of Justiciary in the same way as any other criminal court.

Applications to become a JP are encouraged by the Scottish Government from people of all backgrounds to reflect all parts of the community. By statute, certain people are excluded from serving as a JP – these include:

- individuals at or over the current statutory retirement age for justices of the peace, which is seventy years;
- members of a local council;
- members of the Scottish Parliament;
- members of the House of Commons;
- members of the House of Lords; and
- individuals that have been the subject of sequestration or bankruptcy proceedings.

Successful candidates are those who can demonstrate that they have the necessary personal qualities to become a JP. (Further details are available at: www2.gov.scot/Topics/Justice/law/justice-peace)

## Liability and removal of judges

Judges are historically immune from any civil action brought against them by any disaffected parties – a rule that can be traced back to the time of Viscount Stair. The principal rationale underlying this being that the courts might find themselves awash with claims for compensation from parties unhappy with one aspect or another of a court's decision. It is extremely rare, but not impossible, that members of the judiciary are removed from office for misconduct. In respect of judges in the Court of Session and the High Court of Justiciary, they may be removed from office by the Crown on the recommendation of the First Minister following a resolution of the Scottish Parliament. In order to assuage fears that the right of Parliament to remove judges would inhibit the independence of judges and insert political expediencies into the judicial function, and in order for removal to take place, prior to a parliamentary resolution to this effect, a tribunal must have reported that the judge concerned is unfit for office either by inability, neglect of duty or misbehaviour.

For sheriffs, a similar process applies, whereby the First Minister may issue an order for the removal of a sheriff from office where a tribunal has furnished said sheriff with a report recommending such removal. At the time of writing, two sheriffs have been removed from office: Sheriff Peter Thomson, in 1977, for political activities deemed incompatible with his judicial office; and Sheriff Ewen Stewart, in 1992, who was removed on the grounds of inability under Statutory Instrument No. 1677 (s. 164) of the Sheriff (Removal from Office) Order 1992.

Justices of the peace may be removed from office following a recommendation by the Court of Session to this effect by way of an Act of Sederunt.

## JURORS

Members of the public, sitting as jurors, perform a pivotal role in the Scottish legal system, particularly in criminal matters. The premise behind the role of juries in criminal trials is that if a party has been accused of a criminal matter for which they ought to be punished by society, their guilt should be determined by their peers. The jury is therefore seen as a cornerstone of a civilised criminal justice system. However, as noted in Chapter 3, juries do not sit in less serious, summary criminal trials in the sheriff and district courts, where facts are determined by the judge.

It is worth noting that the jury system has been criticised, particularly in respect of lengthy, technical trials. The suggestion here is that juries may very easily become bamboozled, perplexed and perhaps even bored when faced with a mountain of technical factual and legal argument, which might lead to unsafe, irrational verdicts (see A. Bonnington, 'The stupidest in the world?', (2004) 49 JLSS 12). Reflecting such concerns, the UK Government removed juries from Crown Court trials in England and Wales in complex fraud cases (under ss. 43 and 44 of the Criminal Justice Act 2003). Scotland has not followed suit.

### Jury selection

In Scotland, the jury in a criminal trial comprises fifteen members of the public, selected at random from the electoral register. Following the Criminal Justice and Licensing (Scotland) Act 2010, jurors must have been resident in the United Kingdom for at least the previous five years; be registered electors; and be eighteen years old or over. Those aged over seventy-one have a right to be excused. Certain classes of people are ineligible, including legal professionals and certain ex-offenders; while others are disqualified, including those with mental illness.

The role of the jury is to determine factual matters (and hence, in criminal matters, whether the accused is guilty or not based on the facts presented), with legal matters of the case being decided by the judge. Juries will commonly be given a 'legal direction' by a judge, explaining how the law applies to the case at hand – 'misdirections' in this sense are common grounds for appeal. In criminal cases, a decision can be reached by a simple majority, with the proviso that, for a finding of guilt, eight jurors must have reached that decision (it should be noted that some jurors may have remained undecided). Jurors will appoint a spokesperson who will announce the verdict to the court after a decision has been reached.

On very rare occasions, juries may be present in civil cases in the Court of Session, in which case twelve jurors sit. Again, any civil jury must determine the facts of the case, whereas the law is decided by the judge.

## Essential Facts

- Lawyers in Scotland comprise several distinct professional groups, including solicitors, advocates, solicitor-advocates and licensed conveyancing and executry practitioners.
- Solicitors may be viewed as 'general practitioners' of the law. They fulfil several legal roles and may represent clients in the lower courts.
- Advocates are specialist lawyers who hold rights of audience in the superior Scottish courts and commonly issue opinions (known as 'counsel's opinion') on points of legal interpretation.
- There are various Law Officers of the Crown, including the Lord Advocate, Solicitor General and Advocate General.
- Juries are composed of fifteen members of the public (or twelve members of the public in civil cases) who determine the facts of the case, generally by majority decision.
- There is no separate professional grouping of judges in Scotland. Judges are drawn from the ranks of suitably experienced advocates and solicitors.
- Judges in the superior courts and sheriffs are generally appointed by the Crown, on the advice of the First Minister, who is in turn advised by a Judicial Appointments Board.

## Website resources

**Qualifying as a Scottish solicitor**
Law Society of Scotland
www.lawscot.org.uk/qualifying-and-education/qualifying-as-a-scottish-solicitor/

**What solicitors can do for you**
Law Society of Scotland
www.lawscot.org.uk/for-the-public/what-a-solicitor-can-do-for-you/

**About advocates**
The Faculty of Advocates
www.advocates.org.uk/about-advocates

**Becoming an advocate**
The Faculty of Advocates
www.advocates.org.uk/about-advocates/becoming-an-advocate

**Solicitor advocates**
Law Society of Scotland
www.lawscot.org.uk/members/career-growth/solicitor-advocates/

**Society of Solicitor-Advocates**
SSA
https://solicitoradvocates.org/

**Lord Advocate**
The Scottish Parliament
www.gov.scot/about/who-runs-government/cabinet-and-ministers/lord-advocate/

**Solicitor General**
The Scottish Parliament
www.gov.scot/about/who-runs-government/cabinet-and-ministers/solicitor-general/

**Join the judiciary**
Judicial Appointments Board for Scotland
www.judicialappointments.scot/

**Judiciary of Scotland**
Judiciary of Scotland
www.scotland-judiciary.org.uk/1/0/Home

**Jurors**
SCTS
www.scotcourts.gov.uk/coming-to-court/jurors

### Video resources

**Reflections on the Diploma in Legal Practice PEAT 1**

University of Strathclyde Law School

https://youtu.be/-mhwUIvtraA?list=PL0njE2bWlrR5Mli94csCj
WmRBO9oOeusI

**From devil to advocate**

Faculty of Advocates

https://youtu.be/ceC9CGQSJsY

**Decision in *The Christian Institute and others* v *The Lord Advocate
(Scotland)* [2016] UKSC 51**

UK Supreme Court

https://youtu.be/mtU2WheQfTw

**First Minister Appointment of Law Officers Scottish
Parliament 1 June 2016**

Lawyer TV

https://youtu.be/GDYyIhSrYSY

**Jury selection and attendance**

SCTS Communications

https://youtu.be/9zLC1tWOG7Q

# 6  LEGAL ASSISTANCE FOR THE PUBLIC

Different forms of financial and expert legal assistance are available for members of the public. Some, such as legal aid, are well established, while others, such as university law clinics, are relatively new ways where legal assistance has been developed to meet high levels of public demand.

## LEGAL AID

Legal aid relates to the financial assistance made available by the state to parties, who cannot afford to pay for their own legal representation, to engage lawyers either to represent them in criminal or civil courts or to tender legal advice. Perhaps surprisingly, legal aid for the poor has existed in one form or another since as early as 1424. The modern law of legal aid, however, originated in the aftermath of the Legal Aid and Solicitors (Scotland) Act 1949. The current legal aid scheme is governed by the Legal Aid (Scotland) Act 1986 (as amended) and has been run under the auspices of the Scottish Legal Aid Board since 1987. Until then, its functions were administered by the Law Society of Scotland.

The Scottish Legal Aid Board is headed by a chair and comprises between eleven and fifteen members appointed by the First Minister: two of these must be advocates; two solicitors; one other with experience of the court system; and the remainder lay members. There are two main functions of the Scottish Legal Aid Board: first, to ensure that legal aid is available in accordance with statutory provisions; second, to administer the legal aid fund – a block of money (primarily made up of government grants) from which legal aid fees are paid to legal professionals.

In 2016–17 the Scottish Government's budget allocation for the legal aid fund was £126.1 million. According to the Law Society of Scotland, this was the lowest it has been for well over a decade, and a reduction from the 2015–16 budget by over 7 per cent – from £136.1 million to £126.1 million (see: www.lawscot.org.uk/news-and-events/law-society-news/legal-aid-budget-for-2016-17/).

There are various, distinct species of legal aid available to parties in different circumstances, namely: legal advice and assistance; criminal legal aid; civil legal aid; and legal aid for children's hearings or court hearings connected to a children's hearing.

### Advice and assistance

This state financial assistance pertains to situations where a member of the public is seeking advice and assistance that falls short of representation in court (except for 'Assistance by way of representation' (ABWOR)). In general, legal advice and assistance relates to oral or written advice tendered by a solicitor or advocate either on the application of law to any particular circumstances that have arisen in relation to which the party is seeking advice or as to what legal steps a party might appropriately take, such as the raising of an action in the civil court (or advice regarding whether such advice set out above is required). The advice and assistance scheme covers advice on general legal problems, including:

- divorce, dissolution of a civil partnership, maintenance, or disputes about children;
- contested adoptions;
- preparing for tribunals (e.g., unfair dismissal and social security tribunals);
- preparation before some criminal proceedings;
- making a will; and
- accident claims (e.g., giving advice, preparing a case for criminal injuries compensation and getting medical reports).

There are strict financial criteria for determining the eligibility of a party for advice and assistance. In general, a party will only be eligible for state aid in respect of their legal advice and assistance costs where their 'disposable income' and 'disposable capital' fall below defined statutory levels. Moreover, a sliding scale operates and, in many cases, a contribution towards the fees may be payable by the party receiving the advice. (For current eligibility limits, see: www.slab.org.uk/new-to-legal-aid/eligibility-estimators/)

The right to financial assistance for legal representation in court under ABWOR arises where a party not in custody seeks to tender a guilty plea in court (or change their plea to guilty) and no application for legal aid has yet been made.

### Criminal legal aid

Criminal legal aid is available in respect of appearance in all Scotland's criminal courts. If an accused person is in custody then they may avail themselves of the services of a 'duty solicitor', who will be available at that time. There is no need for any formal application to be made for legal aid to make use of the duty solicitor (provided on a rota by local solicitors) and there will be no enquiry made into the accused person's financial circumstances at this time.

Any accused seeking legal aid for a criminal trial must make a formal application, either to the Scottish Legal Aid Board (in summary cases) or to the court (in solemn cases). Again, the financial status of the accused will be a key factor in determining whether legal aid will be granted. In addition, however, either the Scottish Legal Aid Board or the court may ask several other questions to ascertain eligibility, including:

- Are there any other bodies that might be obliged to meet the legal bill (e.g., a trade union)?
- Is it in the 'interests of justice' that legal aid be granted? This question can further be broken down into several questions, including:
  - Might the finding of guilt lead to loss of liberty or livelihood?
  - Is the evidence complex or the legal issues substantial?
  - Does the defence appear to be frivolous?
  - Is it in the interests of some other person (e.g., the victim) that the accused be represented?

Criminal legal aid is usually granted in the following cases:

- if the accused is likely to go to prison if convicted;
- if the accused is likely to lose their job if convicted;
- if the accused cannot follow what is happening in the trial because of mental or physical disability or because they do not speak English as a first language;
- if the accused has been remanded in custody pending trial; or
- if there is an appeal against a criminal court decision.

Minor offences such as motoring offences are not usually eligible for legal aid.

In recent years, criminal legal aid has been shrouded in controversy. In the 1980s and early 1990s – perhaps the 'golden age' for criminal legal aid practitioners – legal aid was often a lucrative business, as lawyers could charge fees which varied according to the extent of work carried out on each element of their case preparation, travel costs and time spent in court. Escalating fee levels and reported 'sharp practice' by legal professionals (including touting for clients; habitual tendering of not-guilty pleas to maximise revenue before a last-minute shift to an admission of guilt; and excessive, unnecessary case-preparation) eventually led, in 1999, to the introduction of 'fixed fees'. Fixed fees are set amounts that are paid in all summary criminal cases. While fixed fees can be criticised in that they give lawyers a disincentive to prepare a client's case properly and may lead to a two-tier system of justice, which is prejudicial to those who cannot afford to pay for their own lawyers, these arrangements seem a reasonable public response in the face of the hitherto often extravagant sums that criminal legal aid lawyers were drawing from the public purse.

## Civil legal aid

Civil legal aid is available for representation in Scotland's civil courts, several courts of special jurisdiction and some tribunals. Such courts are the Sheriff Court, the Court of Session, the Scottish Land Court and appeals to the UK Supreme Court. Tribunals are the Employment Appeal Tribunal and Lands Tribunal for Scotland. This type of financial assistance is available in respect of most kinds of civil action, with some notable exceptions, including simple procedure in the Sheriff Court (unless the action relates to personal injury) and in certain bankruptcy and diligence proceedings.

Again, in terms of entitlement, the recipient must be financially eligible, the legal action or defence must not be considered spurious, and there should be no other appropriate body that is obliged to meet the bill.

## Legal aid for children

Legal aid is available for children or adults who need advice or representation in relation to a children's hearing or court orders connected to a children's hearing. This type of legal aid is different from civil legal aid and has its own separate rules governed by the Children's Legal Assistance (Scotland) Regulations 2013 (for further details, see: www.slab.org.uk/new-to-legal-aid/eligibility-estimators/estimator-childrens-legal-aid/).

## PUBLIC DEFENCE SOLICITORS' OFFICE

The Public Defence Solicitors' Office (PDSO) was first set up as a pilot project in 1998 under the Crime and Punishment (Scotland) Act 1997, initially for five years, in Edinburgh. The PDSO is a public body that provides lawyers to represent parties in summary criminal matters. Unlike those legal professionals engaged under legal aid, who are private practitioners, public defenders are civil servant solicitors employed by the Scottish Legal Aid Board.

Public defender programmes in other jurisdictions have attracted negative publicity, particularly in the United States, where poor levels of funding, low morale of staff and inadequate services are commonly reported. Moreover, their lack of independence from the state, and who the prosecuting authority is, has been a practical problem as it can lead to the distrust of accused individuals. Initial research on the PDSO in Edinburgh was, nevertheless, at least partially favourable (in terms of, for example, the potential for costs savings and the speedier expediting of cases through the court process; see T. Goriely et al. (2001)). Considering these findings, PDSOs have been rolled out in Glasgow, Edinburgh, Inverness, Ayr, Dundee, Falkirk and Kirkwall.

Whether, in time, PDSOs will ultimately replace the provision of legal aid by the engagement of lawyers in private practice remains to be seen. (For more information about the workings of PDSOs, see: www. pdso.org.uk)

## LAW CENTRES

Law centres are generally non-profit-making concerns, manned by solicitors and paralegals. Law centres seek to fulfil unmet legal requirements in their locality. Perhaps unsurprisingly then, law centres tend to focus on the spheres of law where there is the greatest local need, including consumer disputes, immigration issues, housing problems, employment, criminal injuries compensation, and money and debt. These services are usually offered on a *pro bono* (free) basis to clients.

Law centres are now a common feature of community life in Scotland, particularly in heavily populated, urban areas. Without suggesting exclusivity, examples include Castlemilk Law Centre, Glasgow; Drumchapel Law and Money Advice Centre, Glasgow; East End Community Law Centre, Glasgow; Ethnic Minorities Law Centre, Glasgow; Govan Law Centre, Glasgow; Legal Services Agency, Edinburgh; North Dundee Law Centre; and Paisley Law Centre, among others. Law centres are heavily involved in social justice campaigns, with a huge measure of success in areas as diverse as unfair UK bank charges, the prevention of homelessness, debt law, public law and democracy issues.

Much has been translated into legislation in Scotland, such as the Abolition of Poindings and Warrant Sales Act (2001). Under this Act, it is now illegal to enforce payment of a debt by poinding or warrant sale. Another, the Breastfeeding etc. (Scotland) Act (2005), makes it an offence to prevent or stop a person in charge of a child from feeding that child milk in a public place.

More recently law centres have also had an input into the Property Factors (Scotland) Act (2011). This act established a statutory register of property factors and makes provision for the resolution of disputes between homeowners and property factors.

## CITIZENS' ADVICE BUREAUX

Citizens' Advice bureaux (CA) are local charitable organisations that provide advice and information to members of the public. The sixty-one Citizens' Advice bureaux in Scotland are supported by Citizens Advice Scotland to help them offer advice at 280 service points across the country, from city centres to island communities. In 2018–19 the Citizens Advice Service network helped more than 272,500 clients in Scotland and dealt with almost 744,000 advice issues within the United Kingdom. With support from the network clients in Scotland recouped £134 million thought lost to them.

Citizens' Advice aims to ensure that individuals do not suffer legally or financially due to a lack of knowledge of, or information about, their rights and responsibilities or services available to them, or an inability to express themselves effectively. Much of the work of Citizens' Advice involves tendering free, confidential advice on such matters as money problems and debt control, consumer disputes, benefit entitlement, employment matters and immigration issues.

A relatively recent Citizens' Advice development has been the inception of 'in-court' advisers or lay representatives. These advisers are Citizens' Advice personnel who provide free, in-court support on issues such as small claims, heritable matters, rent arrears and evictions, consumer complaints, debt negotiation and benefits. On occasion, Citizens' Advice advisers may represent client's in court in small claims simple procedure cases. Advisers can often also provide emergency in-court advice and guidance to those who do not have someone to represent them. These services are currently available in six Sheriff Courts in Scotland: Aberdeen; Airdrie; Hamilton; Dundee; Edinburgh and Kilmarnock.

## UNIVERSITY LAW CLINICS

There are currently six university law clinics in Scotland, at Strathclyde, Glasgow Caledonian, Edinburgh, Napier, Aberdeen and Robert Gordon universities. Law clinics are generally run by university law students under the guidance of law staff and external, professionally qualified legal advisers. They offer a free legal-advice service to members of the public. For example, the University of Strathclyde clinic offers advice on a wide range of legal areas, which typically, in practice, focus on consumer complaints, small claims (including representation in court), employment, benefit entitlement claims, and housing and neighbourhood disputes. (For further information about services offered by the Strathclyde law clinic, see: www.lawclinic.org.uk)

## University mediation clinics

An innovation in the field of social justice in Scotland is the University of Strathclyde's Mediation Clinic run under the auspices of its law school. Managed and staffed in much the same way as a university law clinic, the Mediation Clinic helps clients resolve disputes without going to court or a tribunal.

In mediation each party can speak directly to the other and decide if, or by what means, they can settle matters between them. The mediator helps with the discussion so that all interests and concerns can be fully discussed. The mediators do not make decisions; they lead the discussion and look for a way forward that is acceptable to both parties. Mediation can take place at any stage of a dispute and can be effective before or during court action.

There are types of mediations with which the Strathclyde Mediation Clinic cannot help – family and additional support for learning mediation. The University of Strathclyde's Mediation Clinic website points parties towards organisations that specialise in these two areas of conflict resolution. (See: www.strath.ac.uk/humanities/lawschool/mediationclinic/)

## CONCLUSION

Thus ends the fourth edition of *Scottish Legal System Essentials*, the general purpose of which was to update and discuss its history and development, sources of Scots law, the judicial system, alternatives to the court process, legal personnel and legal assistance for the public in Scotland.

I hope you enjoyed reading it as much as I enjoyed writing it.

---

### Essential Facts

- Legal aid is state-provided financial assistance for the engagement of lawyers in private practice for those who cannot afford to pay the legal costs themselves.
- Legal aid is available for legal representation in both the criminal and civil courts and advice and assistance on interpretation of the law or any procedural steps that might be taken in respect of a legal issue.
- The Public Defence Solicitors' Office provides state-employed lawyers who may represent parties in criminal courts and provide legal advice and assistance.

- Citizens' Advice bureaux are voluntary organisations supported by Citizens Advice Scotland that provide free legal advice and assistance on a range of legal issues to members of the public within their local vicinity. A new in-house adviser scheme can provide on-the-spot advice in court.
- Law clinics are staffed by solicitors and support staff who tender legal advice free of charge to the public on a range of legal issues.
- University law clinics are legal advice and assistance services provided for free by university students, who are supervised by solicitors and legal academics.
- A mediation clinic assists members of the public to resolve legal difficulties without going to court. Disputing parties are encouraged by a facilitator to talk through their problem together to arrive at a mutually acceptable solution. Facilitators are called 'mediators' and in a university setting are postgraduate students. They are supported in their practice by experienced mediators and legal academics.

## Website resources

**Legal aid in Scotland**
Legal aid guide
www.mygov.scot/legal-aid
**Public Defence Solicitors' Office**
PDSO
www.pdso.org.uk
**Law Centres in Scotland**
Shelter Scotland
https://scotland.shelter.org.uk/get_advice/advice_topics/complaints_and_court_action/legal_representation/law_centres
**Citizens Advice Scotland**
CAS
www.cas.org.uk

**University law clinics**
Scottish University Law Clinics Network
www.abdn.ac.uk/law/research/the-scottish-university-law-clinic-network-546.php
**University of Strathclyde Law Clinic**
University of Strathclyde
www.lawclinic.org.uk
**University of Strathclyde Mediation Clinic**
University of Strathclyde
www.strath.ac.uk/humanities/lawschool/mediationclinic

## Video resources

**How legal aid can help you**
Scottish Legal Aid Board
https://youtu.be/mZ-8GVgBvqg
**Criminal legal assistance summary cases**
Scottish Legal Aid Board
www.slab.org.uk/videos/criminal-legal-assistance-summary-cases
**Criminal legal assistance solemn cases**
Scottish Legal Aid Board
www.slab.org.uk/videos/criminal-legal-assistance-solemn-cases
**25 Years: Govan Law Centre**
Govan Law Centre
https://youtu.be/14Yp1r6st_A
**Eighty years of Citizens Advice in Scotland**
Citizens Advice Scotland (CAS)
https://youtu.be/KHNep8-B0GY

# GLOSSARY

For ease of reference, although not a comprehensive glossary, definitions of some of the key legal terms used in this book are provided here.

**Accused**: a person accused of a criminal offence

**Act**: expression of will of a parliamentary or law-making body

**Act of Sederunt**: delegated legislation whereby the courts may enact rules regarding court procedure

**Action**: proceedings commenced in a civil court

**Adjudication**: (1) a form of diligence over heritable property; (2) a special truncated form of dispute resolution in construction disputes

**Admonition**: a sentence handed out by a criminal court that amounts to a warning

**Adversarialism**: type of court process prevalent in Scotland, where each side presents its own case of fact and law and the court decides in favour of one party

**Advocate**: a legal professional who traditionally has rights of audience in the higher courts

**Advocate General**: (1) Law Officer of the Crown who is the legal adviser to the UK Government on issues pertaining to Scotland; (2) court official of the European Court of Justice who issues an opinion on the case at hand to the judges

**Alternative Dispute Resolution (ADR)**: alternatives to the court process for the resolution of civil disputes and criminal cases

**Appeal**: appealing a court or tribunal decision on either the facts, a point of law or some procedural irregularity

**Appellant**: party making an appeal

**Arbiter**: the party engaged to settle a dispute in arbitration

**Arbitration**: an alternative to the court process where parties engage an arbiter to resolve a dispute

**Attachment**: a form of diligence over moveable property in the hands of the debtor

**Attorney General**: Law Officer of the Crown who advises the UK Government on legal issues

**Award**: decision given by an arbiter in arbitration

**Bail**: being released from custody pending a trial

**Bar**: the collective name for the advocacy profession

**Bicameral**: a parliamentary system with two legislative houses (e.g., the House of Commons and the House of Lords, or the Senate and the House of Representatives in the United States)

**Bill**: an expression of parliamentary intent

**Bill of Advocation**: right of appeal in the criminal courts, made because of some procedural irregularity by the prosecutor

**Bill of Suspension**: right of appeal in the criminal courts, made because of some procedural irregularity by the defence

**Byelaw**: delegated legislation passed by a local authority

**Case Law**: decisions of the courts

**Case Management**: a process by which courts attempt to take control of, and speed up, the timetabling of different aspects of the court process

**Civil Law**: (1) law that generally regulates relationships between private parties (i.e., non-criminal); (2) law which is derived historically from Roman law

**Codifying Act**: an Act which brings into statute previous common law principles which have governed an area

**(The) Commission**: executive body of the European Union

**Common Law**: (1) law which has developed from non-statutory sources; (2) law that is drawn in a historical sense from English law

**Community Service**: sentence of the criminal courts whereby an offender must carry out free work in the community

**Complainer**: victim in a criminal case

**Complaint**: document setting out criminal charges in a summary case

**Confidence and Supply**: A confidence and supply agreement sees one political party in either the Westminster or Holyrood Parliaments agree to support another in matters of confidence and finance (supply)

**Consolidation Act**: an Act which brings together several other Acts in the same place

**Constitutional Convention**: a non-binding, customary rule of the constitution

**(The) Council**: main legislative body of the European Union

**Court of Session**: Scotland's highest civil court

**Court of the First Instance**: court within the European Court of Justice that often deals with cases in the first instance

**Court of the Lord Lyon**: court dealing with heraldry, the right to bear arms and the use of clan badges

**Courts Martial**: UK-wide courts that have been established within the armed forces to deal with military disciplinary matters

**Criminal Law**: law that sets out a minimum level of societal conduct

**Damages**: remedy provided by civil courts that amounts to financial compensation

**Declaratory Act**: an Act designed to re-state the law, often in the aftermath of an unpopular or inconvenient court decision

**Decree**: judgment given by a civil court

**Defences**: statement by way of defence lodged by a defender in a civil action

**Defender**: party defending a civil action

**Delegated Legislation**: legislation enacted where the right to legislate has been delegated by Parliament to some other person or body

**Devolution**: the process by which powers were vested upon the Scottish Parliament from the UK Parliament

**Devolved Areas**: spheres of law in which the Scottish Parliament is competent to enact legislation

**Diet**: a court hearing

**Diligence**: a process by which creditors can enforce the payment of court debts by the 'freezing' and sometimes sale of the debtor's assets

**Diligence Over Earnings**: diligence over the earnings of the debtor

**District Court**: was the lowest court in the criminal hierarchy in Scotland until the Criminal Proceedings etc. (Reform) (Scotland) Act 2007 when its functions were transferred to the Justice of the Peace Courts

**Employment Appeal Tribunal**: body that hears appeals from employment tribunals

**Employment Tribunal**: a body that settles civil disputes arising in the employment sphere

**Equity**: process by which the law may be softened in practice in Scotland (e.g., by way of equitable court remedies)

**European Court of Human Rights**: court enforcing provisions of the European Convention on Human Rights against states which are signatories thereto

**European Court of Justice**: court of the European Union

**European Parliament**: principally an advisory body in the EC law-making process

**Faculty of Advocates**: governing body for advocates

**Fatal Accident Inquiry**: state-mandated inquiry held in the aftermath of a fatal accident

**Feudalism**: system of landownership in which all land vests in the Crown and is granted to other tenants in return for feu duties

**Feu Duty**: service rendered in return for granting of land

**First Minister**: head of the Scottish Government

**Fiscal Fine**: financial penalty payable in minor crime instead of prosecution through the courts

**Formal Source**: source of law which renders a legal rule binding

**Full Bench**: a sitting of the High Court of Justiciary consisting of more than the minimum number of judges required to hear an appeal

**(Action of) Furthcoming**: a procedure by which items subject to diligence may be brought to auction and sold

**Golden Rule**: rule of statutory interpretation where courts will interpret statutes in a literal fashion, except where this would give rise to an absurd result

**Green Paper**: government expression of legislative intent issued for consultation

**Intervention** is a procedure to allow a non-party, called an 'intervenor', to join ongoing litigation, either as a matter of right or at the discretion of the court, without the permission of the original litigants – the rationale for intervention is that a judgment in a case may affect the rights of non-parties, who ideally should have the right to be heard

**Hereditary Peer**: member of the House of Lords by virtue of historical birthright

**High Court of Justiciary**: highest criminal court in Scotland

**House of Commons**: elected chamber of UK Parliament

**House of Lords**: non-elected, second Chamber of UK Parliament

**Indictment**: document setting out criminal charges that an accused will face under solemn procedure

**Inhibition**: a form of diligence over heritable property

**Inner House**: the appeal court within the Court of Session

**Institutional Writer**: eminent legal jurist whose writings came to be regarded as a valid formal source of law (e.g., Viscount Stair)

**Interdict**: civil court decree which prohibits a party from taking some course of action

**Interim Interdict**: civil court decree which prohibits a party from taking some course of action pending full resolution of the case

**Judicial Precedent**: process by which court decisions become binding on subsequent ones

**Judicial Review**: process by which action of public bodies can be reviewed in the court

**Junior Counsel**: a lower-ranked advocate who is not yet a QC (senior counsel)

**Jury**: members of the public who determine the facts of cases in both criminal and (rarely) civil cases

**Justiciars**: historical judicial figures who represented the Crown

**Justice of the Peace**: non-legally qualified judge in a Justice of the Peace Court

**Lands Tribunal for Scotland**: tribunal with a statutory power to deal with various types of dispute involving land or property

**Lands Valuation Appeal Court**: court that hears appeals from decisions of local valuation appeal committees and the Scottish Lands Tribunal

**Law Society of Scotland**: regulatory body for solicitors

**Lawyer**: a general term for a legal professional

**Lay**: denotes that a party is not legally qualified (e.g., a Citizens Advice lay-representative)

**Legal Aid**: state financial assistance for the provision of legal advice, assistance and representation

**Liberal Rule**: rule of statutory interpretation in which statutes are interpreted in a liberal way to afford them the meaning that Parliament is taken to have intended

**Life Peer**: appointed member of the House of Lords

**Literal Rule**: rule of statutory interpretation in which statutes are interpreted in a strict to-the-letter fashion

**Litigation**: civil court proceedings

**Lord Advocate**: head of the prosecution service in Scotland and member of the Scottish Government

**Lord Justice-Clerk**: depute to Lord President (and Lord Justice-General) in Scotland's superior courts

**Lord Justice-General**: head judge in the High Court of Justiciary (same person as Lord President)

**Lord Ordinary**: judge in the Outer House of the Court of Session

**Lord President**: Scotland's senior judge (heads both the High Court of Justiciary and the Court of Session)

**Lords of Appeal in Ordinary**: judges who sit in the Judicial Committee of the House of Lords

**Lords of Session**: judges in the Inner House of the Court of Session

**Lords Superior**: under the feudal system, noblemen who received land directly from a Crown grant

**Mediation**: process by which parties may resolve their dispute with the assistance of a neutral third party

**Mediator**: neutral third party in mediation

**Messenger-at-arms**: executes criminal and civil processes (including diligence) in the Court of Session and the High Court of Justiciary

**Mischief Rule**: rule of statutory interpretation in which statutes are interpreted in a liberal fashion to ensure that the Act deals with the legal issue that it was enacted to resolve

*Nobile Officium*: equitable power of the High Court of Justiciary and the Court of Session to provide remedies where the law does not provide one

*Obiter Dicta*: judicial comments in a court judgment not directly relevant to resolution of the case – these are never binding in subsequent cases

**Ombudsman**: official who may investigate public complaints in both the public and private sectors

**Ordinary Cause**: civil court procedure in the Sheriff Court for actions involving more than £5,000

**Outer House**: the court of first instance within the Court of Session

**Oversman**: party appointed to give award in arbitration where the two arbiters appointed by the parties cannot agree

**Petition**: (1) process by which a party may petition a civil court for a remedy; (2) document which sets out initial charges and commences criminal proceedings in solemn procedure

**Petitioner**: party bringing a petition in the civil courts

**Plea in Bar of Trial**: a preliminary plea brought prior to the trial diet in criminal matters

**Pleadings**: legal arguments lodged in court in a civil action

**Poinding**: to take the property of a debtor

**Precognition**: interview of witnesses in a criminal case by either the prosecution or the defence

**Presiding Officer**: official in the Scottish Parliament whose remit is to ensure the effective and lawful nature of business in the House

**Private Bill**: a Bill promoted by individuals or groups that are generally seeking some sort of benefit for themselves

**Private Law**: law which pertains to relations between private parties (rather than the state)

**Private Member's Bill**: a Bill brought by a Member of Parliament who is not a member of the Government

**Privy Council**: the Judicial Committee of the Privy Council is the court of final appeal for UK overseas territories and Crown dependencies, and for those Commonwealth countries that have retained the appeal to Her Majesty in Council or, in the case of Republics, to the Judicial Committee

**Probation**: a criminal sentence imposed by the court that amounts to a good behaviour bond

**Procurator Fiscal**: responsible for prosecuting offenders on a local basis

**Public Bill**: a Bill which will apply to the nation in general (e.g., general Acts of Parliament derive from Public Bills)

**Public Defenders**: state-employed lawyers who provide legal assistance and representation for accused persons who cannot afford their own lawyers

**Public Law**: law which pertains to the relationship of the state with members of the public

**Pursuer**: the party raising a civil action against another

**QC**: Queen's Counsel; a senior advocate

*Ratio Decidendi*: the rationale that was central to the decision in a previous case which may become binding in subsequent cases

**Record**: the statement of legal arguments and responses by the parties lodged in court in a civil action. While adjustments by the parties are being made the record is said to be 'open'; when the adjustments are finalised, the record is 'closed'

**Respondent**: successful party in a civil action where the other party is appealing

**Restrictive Practices Court**: UK-wide court that hears cases relating to monopolies, unfair pricing practices and price maintenance agreements

**Right of Way**: right of access over land which can arise by usage over time

**Rights of Audience**: rights to appear and represent parties in court

**Royal Assent**: monarch's 'rubber-stamping' of Acts of Parliament

**Scottish Law Commission**: body that examines areas of law on behalf of government

**Senior Counsel**: a senior advocate (QC)

**Sheriff**: judge in the Sheriff Court

**Sheriff-clerk**: civil servant who provides clerical assistance to sheriff

**Sheriff Court**: court with wide civil and criminal jurisdiction

**Sheriffdom**: area in which the sheriff principal exercises jurisdiction

**Sheriff Officer**: executes criminal and civil processes (including diligence) in the Sheriff Court

**Sheriff Principal**: head sheriff in sheriffdom; hears appeals from sheriffs in civil matters

**Small Claim**: truncated civil court procedure in the Sheriff Court now under simple procedure, where the amount of claim is below £3,000

**Solicitor**: general practitioner of the law

**Solicitor-advocate**: solicitor who has obtained extended rights of audience to appear in the superior courts in Scotland

**Solicitor General**: depute to the Lord Advocate

**Special Defence**: technical defences that can be mounted by an accused: insanity, incrimination, alibi and self-defence

**Specific Implement**: civil court remedy in which a party is ordered to do something

***Stare Decisis***: standing by (court) decisions

**Stated Case**: appeal procedure by which the judge at first instance must state the grounds for their decision, which may then be reviewed by the appeal court

**Statutory Instrument**: delegated legislation made by a Government Minister

**Statutory Interpretation**: process by which a court (or lawyer) interprets legislation and applies it to a given set of facts

**Statutory Law**: law which is derived from legislation

**Stipendiary Magistrate**: were judges in district courts in Glasgow; abolished under the Courts Reform (Scotland) Act 2014 with the creation of the new post of summary sheriff

**Summary Cause**: form of civil court procedure in the Sheriff Court where the value of dispute is between £3,000 and £5,000, and for actions pertaining to recovery of possession of heritable property

**Summary Procedure**: procedure for minor criminal offences in either the district or Sheriff Court (there is no jury in summary cases)

**Summary Sheriff:** hears civil cases brought under simple procedure and criminal cases brought under summary proceedings – their sentencing powers are identical to a sheriff sitting in summary proceedings

**Tribunal**: forum in which certain civil disputes can be resolved as an alternative to the court process

**Unicameral**: a parliamentary system in which there is only one legislative chamber (e.g., as found in New Zealand with the New Zealand single-chamber Parliament)

**Vassal**: recipient of land from a lord superior under the feudal system

**White Paper**: government expression of parliamentary intent published for public consultation

# FURTHER READING

## Chapter 1

Meston and Sellar, *The Scottish Legal Tradition* (1991)

*The Laws of Scotland: Stair Memorial Encyclopaedia*, vol. 22, 'Sources of Law'

Walker, *A Legal History of Scotland*, vols 1–6 (1988–2001)

Walker, *The Scottish Legal System* (8th edn, 2001)

White, Willock and MacQueen, *The Scottish Legal System* (5th edn, 2013)

## Chapter 2

Ashton and Finch, *Constitutional Law in Scotland* (2000)

Ashton and Finch, *Administrative Law in Scotland* (2001)

*Butterworths Core Text: European Union Law* (5th edn, 2008)

Buxton, 'The Human Rights Act and Private Law' (2000) 116 LQR 48

Craig and de Búrca, *EU Law Text, Cases and Materials* (6th edn, 2015)

Dewart, *The Scottish Legal System* (6th edn, 2019)

Gloag and Henderson, *The Law of Scotland* (14th edn, 2017)

Himsworth and O'Neill, *Constitutional Law in Scotland* (2003)

Himsworth and O'Neill, *Scotland's Constitution: Law and Practice* (3rd edn, 2015)

Horspool, Humphreys and Wells-Greco, *European Union Law* (Core Texts Series) (6th edn, 2018)

*The Laws of Scotland: Stair Memorial Encyclopaedia*, vol. 22, 'Sources of Law (Formal)'

McFadden and Lazarowicz, *The Scottish Parliament: An Introduction* (4th edn, 2010)

Paterson, Bates and Poustie, *The Legal System of Scotland: Cases and Materials* (4th edn, 1999)

Reed and Murdoch, *A Guide to Human Rights Law in Scotland* (3rd edn, 2011)

Reed and Murdoch, *Human Rights Law in Scotland* (4th edn, 2016)

Scottish Government, *Making Justice Work. Enabling Access to Justice Project – Overview Report of Alternative Dispute Resolution in Scotland* (2014)

Starmer, 'Two years of the Human Rights Act' (2003) 1 EHRLR 14

Walker, *The Scottish Legal System* (8th edn, 2001)

Wade, 'The United Kingdom's Bill of Rights', in Hare and Forsyth (eds), *Constitutional Reform in the UK: Practice and Principles* (1998)

White and Willock, *The Scottish Legal System* (4th edn, 2007)

## Chapter 3

Auchie, *Summary Cause Procedure in the Sheriff Court* (2nd edn, 2004)

Brown, *Criminal Evidence and Procedure: An Introduction* (3rd edn, 2010)

Gloag and Henderson, *The Law of Scotland* (14th edn, 2017)

Gretton, 'Striking the Balance: Warrant Sales: At the Turning Point', 2001 SLT (News) 30, 255–8

Kelbie, *Small Claims Procedure in the Sheriff Court* (1994)

*The Laws of Scotland: Stair Memorial Encyclopaedia*, vol. 6, 'Courts and Competency', 'The House of Lords', 'The High Court of Justiciary', 'The Court of Session', 'The Sheriff Court' and 'The District Court' MacPherson, 'Warrant Sales: At the Turning Point', 2001 SLT (News) 35, 289–92

Paterson, Bates and Poustie, *The Legal System of Scotland: Cases and Materials* (4th edn, 1999)

White, Willock and MacQueen, *The Scottish Legal System* (5th edn, 2013)

## Chapter 4

Bennett, 'The role of workplace mediation: a critical assessment', in *Personnel Review*, (2014) 43(5), 764–79

Clark, 'Institutionalising Mediation', 2008 JR 193

Clark, *Lawyers and Mediation* (2012)

Davidson, *Arbitration* (2nd edn, 2012)

Davidson, 'Some thoughts on the Draft Arbitration (Scotland) Bill', 2009 JBL 44

Hunter, *The Law of Arbitration in Scotland* (2nd edn, 2002)

Kearney, *Children's Hearings and the Sheriff Court* (2nd edn, 2000)

Kearney, *Children's Hearings (Scotland) Act 2011* (Greens Annotated Acts) (2016)

Macauley, 'Adjudication: Rough Justice?', 2000 SLT (News) 217

McIvor et al., *Establishing Drug Courts in Scotland: Early Experiences of the Pilot Drug Courts in Glasgow and Fife* (Scottish Executive Research Report, 2003)

Malcolm and O'Donnell, *A Guide to Mediating in Scotland* (2009)

Mays and Clark, *Alternative Dispute Resolution in Scotland* (Scottish Office Central Research Unit Report, 1999)

Moody and Mackay (eds), *Greens Guide to Alternative Dispute Resolution in Scotland* (1995)

Norrie, *Children's Hearings in Scotland* (3rd edn, 2013)

Norrie, 'Human Rights Challenges to the Children's Hearing System', (2000) 4 JLSS 8

Samuel, *Supporting Court Users: The In-court Advice and Mediation Projects in Edinburgh Sheriff Court* (Scottish Executive Report (phase 2), 2002)

Scottish Legal Action Group, 'Civil justice reform: modernising the civil justice system in Scotland', (2005) 331 SCOLAG 101

## Chapter 5

Dewart and MacQueen, *Studying Scots Law* (5th edn, 2016)

*The Laws of Scotland: Stair Memorial Encyclopaedia*, vol. 13, 'Legal Profession, Solicitors' and 'The Modern Faculty of Advocates'

Walker, *The Scottish Legal System* (8th edn, 2001)

## Chapter 6

Goriely et al., *The Public Defence Solicitors' Office in Edinburgh: an independent evaluation* (Scottish Executive Central Research Unit Report, 2001)

## Glossary

O'Rourke and Duncan, *Glossary of Scottish Legal Terms* (4th edn, 2004)

# INDEX

EU representative:
Easy Access System Europe
Mustamäe tee 50, 10621 Tallinn, Estonia
Gpsr.requests@easproject.com

www.ingramcontent.com/pod-product-compliance
Lightning Source LLC
Chambersburg PA
CBHW070352200326
41518CB00012B/2216